Generation Hex

Generation Hex

Dillon Burroughs
Marla Alupoaicei

HARVEST HOUSE PUBLISHERS
EUGENE, OREGON

Cover by Left Coast Design, Portland, Oregon

Cover photo © Kamil Vojnar / Photonica / Getty Images; Author photo of Marla Alupoaicei by Tammy Labuda / back-cover author photo of Dillon Burroughs by Josiah Goff

GENERATION HEX
Copyright © 2008 by Dillon Burroughs and Marla Alupoaicei
Published by Harvest House Publishers
Eugene, Oregon 97402
www.harvesthousepublishers.com

Library of Congress Cataloging-in-Publication Data
    Burroughs, Dillon.
    Generation hex / Dillon Burroughs and Marla Alupoaicei.
        p. cm.
    Includes bibliographical references.
    ISBN-13: 978-0-7369-2401-6 (pbk.)
    ISBN-10: 0-7369-2401-9 (pbk.)
    1. Wicca. 2. Witchcraft. I. Alupoaicei, Marla, 1974- II. Title.
    BP605.W53B87 2008
    261.2'994—dc22

                                                            2008012048

Printed in the United States of America

08 09 10 11 12 13 14 15 16 / VP-SK / 10 9 8 7 6 5 4 3 2 1

Contents

Foreword

by Ron Rhodes

You may have encountered Wiccans in the course of day-to-day living without even knowing they were Wiccans. (There are lots of them out there—some perhaps living in your neighborhood.) You've likely witnessed the huge Wicca section at mainstream bookstores such as Barnes & Noble—and this is aside from the prominent displays of the mega-bestselling Harry Potter novels. You've also no doubt come across some of the popular TV shows on witches—*Charmed*, *Sabrina the Teenage Witch*, and *Buffy the Vampire Slayer* come to mind. Wicca has obviously penetrated the popular culture—big time!

As an adjunct professor of Christian apologetics at Dallas Theological Seminary, Southern Evangelical Seminary, and Biola University, I have for years taught college and graduate-level courses about Wicca and other alternative religions that now pepper the religious landscape in America. This requires that I read hundreds upon hundreds of articles and books on the subject. Every once in a while, I am pleasantly surprised to discover a true jewel of a book. *Generation Hex*, by Marla Alupoaicei and Dillon Burroughs, is one such book.

You have probably noticed that we are witnessing a wave of neopaganism crashing upon the shores of contemporary Western thought and life. The need of the day is for an accurate description of this phenomenon, based on firsthand research, coupled with a thoughtful critique that is communicated with a compassionate heart. *Generation Hex* is custom-designed to meet the need.

Alupoaicei and Burroughs have managed to sift through mountains of data in their research, while in the book focusing only on the most important details so that (thankfully) readers do not get bogged down in the extraneous. The book uses nontechnical and easy-to-understand language as it answers such questions as: Are all Wiccans witches? Are all witches Wiccans? How can you tell if a person is a witch? Why is Wicca so appealing to women? What types of spells and rituals do pagans perform? How can I create open dialogue with a person of a pagan faith?

Some Christian critiques I've read on Wicca have unfortunately presented a false caricature of the craft, and then provided substantial argumentation against that false caricature. Alupoaicei and Burroughs, by contrast, have jettisoned false stereotypes and gone to great lengths to fairly and accurately represent the beliefs and practices of Wiccans. Indeed, they have personally *interviewed* Wiccans—and one entire chapter in the book is even written by a former Wiccan who is now a Christian ("I Was a Witch").

While Alupoaicei and Burroughs—both graduates of Dallas Theological Seminary—provide substantive biblical reasons why Wiccans ought to rethink their position and turn to the Jesus of the Bible for a truly liberating spirituality, they do so in a friendly, positive, and engaging way. While they speak authoritatively, they are never derogatory or inflammatory, seeking always to be faithful to the biblical injunction to defend the truth "with gentleness and respect" (1 Peter 3:15). By taking this approach, the authors effectively teach Christians how to build an evangelistic bridge between Christianity and Wicca.

Make no mistake about it. This book is not just about *exposing darkness*. It's also about *lighting a candle* in the midst of the darkness, recognizing that Jesus has called each of us as Christians to be a light in our world (Matthew 5:13-16). By the time you get to the last page of this book, you will be able to intelligently and compassionately engage Wiccans in an open dialogue, and communicate to them both what you believe and why you believe it.

I am confident God will use *Generation Hex* to deliver many from the futile quest for spirituality without the guidance of the biblical gospel. That is my prayer.

—Dr. Ron Rhodes
Author of over 40 books (most of which deal
with unbiblical alternative spiritualities)

PART ONE

WHAT IS WICCA?

Wicca 101

What Is It? Why Should I Care?

❦

"Wicca is the fastest-growing religion in America."
—Phyllis Curott, Wiccan High Priestess[1]

A girl on the bus cast a spell on me today," Jill (not her real name) informed me.[2] I (Dillon) thought she was joking. Sure, I had seen the spell books at Barnes & Noble and had even heard about the voodoo doll kits and Ouija boards that could be bought at our local department stores. But Jill was just kidding, right?

She wasn't. In fact, her spell-casting bus companion was not the typical black-clad, black-nail-polish-wearing Goth stereotype from the fringes of the teenage social scene. Rather, she was one of the popular girls who wore the latest designer fashions from Abercrombie & Fitch and Hollister. Yet this same girl carried crystals, drew pictures of pentacles and other religious symbols in her notebooks, and chatted with a few older friends online about an alternative belief system known as Wicca.

This encounter took place seven years ago. And it represented only the beginning of my experiences with this belief system.

You might think that for me—at that time a pastor to teenagers and college students in suburban Dallas, Texas—Wicca and witchcraft would be at the bottom of the list of troubling teenage issues I confronted. However, among the students I served, the number-one religion I encountered other than Christianity was not Islam or Judaism, but Wicca. Even during the post–9/11 months, when understanding Islam was at the forefront of most people's minds, the average suburban teenager was also facing questions about divination, reincarnation, spell-casting, potion-making, and a blending of spiritual beliefs that challenged the values many teenagers had been taught at home and at church.

Yet, despite the explosion of interest in Wicca among today's teenagers, the most common question we continue to get from parents and other adults is, "What exactly *is* Wicca?" Either they haven't heard of it, or they didn't realize it was such a big deal in today's culture.

AMERICA'S MOST POPULAR FORM *of* WITCHCRAFT

Studies confirm that Wicca is the fastest-growing religion in America. By some estimates, it will become America's third-largest religion by 2012 (after Christianity and Judaism). According to Wiccan high priestess and bestselling author Phyllis Curott, between three and five million Wiccans lived in the United States by the end of 1999.[3] If Curott's predictions of the continued growth of Wicca are accurate, it may even become America's second-largest religion—and most people don't even know what it is.[4]

If you find yourself in the "What exactly *is* Wicca?" category (or maybe even the "Why should I care?" category), this book is for you.

What Is Wicca?

Wicca, sometimes called "the Craft" or "the Craft of the Wise," has emerged as the most popular form of today's many earth-based religions and forms of witchcraft. One of its major tenets is this philosophy:

An it harm none, do as you will.

(In contemporary English, this means, "As long as it doesn't hurt anyone else, do whatever you want.")

With this appealing credo, Wicca has exploded onto the American religious scene. It's particularly widespread among children, teenagers, and young adults. A 2004 *Religion Link* article notes that "Wicca has enchanted pop culture and many teenagers."[5]

Steve Wohlberg, author of *The Hour of the Witch*, writes, "Witchcraft is growing so fast on high school and college campuses that Wiccan visionaries are rushing to establish their own schools."[6] Chas Clifton, editor of *Pomegranate: The International Journal of Pagan Studies*, echoes Wohlberg's words: "We [Pagans] are like a third world country that can't put up enough elementary schools fast enough."[7] Pagans and Christians agree that Wicca is becoming a major religious educational force in America.

Many Wiccans seeking training turn to WitchSchool.com on the internet. This is not simply a small informational site—it's a full-fledged witch school with over 130,000 students, a staff of over 300, and every online tool used by major universities.

According to the president of WitchSchool.com, Davron Michaels,

> The school is an important part of the emerging healthy community that can provide the needed training for services and duties required of our members. Right now that mission includes helping the over one hundred new students a day that join us to get their quality understanding of the basics of Wicca. We are providing education at every level for thousands of Witches worldwide. It is a sacred trust that we are faced with every day.[8]

Another organization, the Church and School of Wicca, claims to have introduced more than 200,000 people to the craft. In addition, it publishes the longest-running Wiccan newsletter (called *Survival*), and has even helped in the development of Wiccan chaplain handbooks for state prison systems.[9]

In North Carolina, another Wiccan group promotes its yearly Vacation Witchcraft School alongside Christian Vacation Bible

Schools in the local newspaper.[10] This same group is listed on the well-known Wicca website Witchvox.com as the Appalachian Pagan Alliance. This group also organized the "We Still Work Magic" rally in 2000, held at a public high school in protest of the Christian "We Still Pray" school prayer rally that was held there the month before. The pagan event drew over 400 participants and received national media coverage from MSNBC, the Associated Press, and dozens of newspapers, radio stations, and television networks all across the country.[11]

Why the increased interest in Wicca and witchcraft among today's children and teenagers? Many factors have contributed to the rise of interest, but today's popular media stories are certainly a key area of influence. For another, try this exercise at your nearest Barnes & Noble or Borders bookstore next time you visit. First, find the "Religion" or "Christianity" section. Then step over to the next row. Where are you standing? In an *entire row* of books categorized as "New Age" or "Witchcraft."

The vast majority of books on popular spirituality target Wicca, with titles like *Wicca: A Guide for the Solitary Practitioner* (400,000-plus sold) now reaching bestseller status. Wicca's acceptance can be seen everywhere—from public schools to the U.S. military, federal prisons, local hospitals, local bookstores, and even some local churches.

A second highly influential book on Wicca for teenagers, available at most bookstores, is *Teen Witch: Wicca for a New Generation* by Silver RavenWolf. RavenWolf, described as "one of the most famous witches in the world today," has published an entire line of books to assist young Wiccan practitioners in casting spells, creating potions, and even building altars for their own witchcraft practices. Other witchcraft titles, such as *Sons of the Goddess: A Young Man's Guide to Wicca* and *Wicca for Couples*, are available at local retailers.

The Minnesota-based company Llewellyn is the world's oldest and largest New Age publisher, specializing in an array of witchcraft-related books, tarot decks, and audio and video products. The

Llewellyn website includes articles such as "Craft Your Own Book of Shadows" and "An Essential Guide to Successful Witchery."[12] The teen section alone contains 66 products. But Llewellyn is not the only player in the market. When you consider the recent influx of Wicca- and witchcraft-related fiction targeted toward today's youth, it's impossible to ignore witchcraft's prominence in our culture.

The most famous fiction series today (and the bestselling fiction series of all time) is the Harry Potter books. At the time of this writing, after the release of seven books and five blockbuster Hollywood films, author J.K. Rowling is Britain's richest woman and the first-ever billionaire author. Harry Potter literature "is now a regular feature of the academy, taught alongside Shakespeare, Dickens and Faulkner."[13]

TOURING HARRY'S WORLD

In May 2007, the Universal Orlando Resort in Orlando, Florida, announced the construction of the Wizarding World of Harry Potter, a 20-acre theme park scheduled to open in 2009.

While fans wait for Wizarding World to open, they can attend one of numerous Potter festivals held in such places as Wilmington, Ohio; Baraboo, Wisconsin; Poulsbo, Washington; Oshkosh, Wisconsin; and Oak Park, Illinois. Each of these cities has hosted celebrations that have attracted over 10,000 people.

In addition, an entire industry of related novels has been developed for the readers of the Harry Potter series. When I stopped by the children's book section at an Indiana Books-A-Million store, I found an entire table of witchcraft and sorcery-related titles for children, both fiction and nonfiction, with a sign that read, "For Fans of Harry Potter." Other bookstores and retailers utilize similar marketing practices.

Some of the more popular releases with witchcraft-related themes include the following:

+ The Sweep Series by Cate Tiernan. It includes the titles *Blood Witch*, *Dark Magick*, and *Spellbound*, all focused on the power of Wicca.

+ *Wizardology* by Master Merlin and Dugald A. Steer. This number-one New York Times bestselling book includes this publisher description: "*Wizardology* offers valuable spells, charms, recipes, arcane wisdom, and even helpful tips: 'For the chasing away of boils, buboes, pustules and unsightly lumps.' But, Apprentices, beware and take heed: '*Wizardology* is not a subject to be pottered with. Heed the example of Dr. Faustus, who made an ill-advised pact with a rather nasty spirit. He got everything he wanted but had to pay with his soul.'"

+ The Septimus Heap Series. This series features a young boy, Septimus Heap, discovering his calling as a wizard and learning the fine arts of conjuring spirits, casting spells, and performing other feats of magick in books with titles like *Magyk*, *Flyte*, and *Physik*.

As of this writing, the Top 10 list at Amazon.com includes five titles related to the subject of witchcraft. That's half of the bestselling books in America![14]

Other signs of Wicca's acceptance into mainstream culture include the following:

+ The 2006 gathering of the Council for a Parliament of the World's Religions in Barcelona included 60 Wiccan and neopagan participants, more than ever before. In 2003, the first neopagan, a Wiccan, was elected to the council's board of trustees.

+ Pagan Pride Day, usually held in late September, has seen its celebrations grow from 18 attendees in 1998 to 117 this year.

+ The Covenant of Unitarian Universalist Pagans (CUUPS), a group of Wiccans and other neopagans within the Unitarian Universalist church, has grown to 70 chapters in 36 states.

+ Wiccans and neopagans have their own seminary in Bethel, Vermont.

+ The number of academics who study Wicca and other forms of neopaganism has grown to the point that they plan to seek formal recognition as a group from the American Academy of Religion.

+ Spiral Scouts International, a Boy and Girl Scout–like orga- nization for children of pagan and other minority religions, now has "circles" of little Wiccans and other neopagans in 22 states.

+ In Puyallup, Washington, officials cancelled Halloween school celebrations out of concern that witch costumes and decorations might be offensive to local Wiccans.[15]

+ Studies show a marked rise in the number of pagan home- schooling networks, many of which use resources such as the book *Pagan Homeschooling* by Kristin Madden.

Why Should I Care?

Even when we describe the skyrocketing popularity of Wicca and explain some of the dangers it poses, people often ask, "So what if Wicca is popular? Is there any reason why I should be concerned?"

Yes, you have reason for concern—especially if you're a parent, a pastor, a youth pastor, a teacher, or have any contact with or concern for young people. A 2006 survey by Christian researcher George Barna reveals that three out of every four teenagers have engaged in at least one type of psychic or witchcraft-related activity. Among the most common endeavors? Using a Ouija board, reading books about witchcraft or Wicca, playing games involving sorcery or witchcraft, having a "professional" do a palm reading, and having one's fortune told.

Specifically, 30 percent of the over 4000 teenagers surveyed had had their palm read, 27 percent had visited a fortune-teller, and 9 per- cent had consulted a spirit guide or a psychic. Even more shocking,

10 percent of teenagers in the study claimed to have communicated with a dead person.[16]

The research also revealed that

> many churches fail to address the subject of the super-natural with sufficient frequency or relevance...Only one-quarter of church teenagers (28 percent) recall receiving any teaching at their church in the last year that helped to shape their views on the supernatural world![17]

Yet another Barna survey discovered that only 4 out of 100 churches had provided *any spiritual training* about the themes and content of the Harry Potter books.[18]

The major concern resulting from the surge in popularity of Wicca and witchcraft is the effect this pagan influence will have on the spiritual beliefs and behaviors of teenagers, their friends and families, and the community and cultures they live in.

We should care because the popular teachings of Wicca and witchcraft are influencing the foundational beliefs of today's generation. As a teenager or college student, you should care because these influences are most dominant among your generation. As a parent, pastor, or teacher, you should care because your children and students are increasingly encountering these beliefs and practices in their schools, among their friends, and in the media.

Welcome to *Generation Hex*—an investigation of today's meteoric rise of Wicca and other forms of witchcraft. We believe you'll be surprised by the widespread influence of Wicca and motivated to evaluate your own spirituality in light of today's trends.

The Harry Potter Factor

Wicca's Popularity

> *"There can be no doubt that television, the movies, and the Internet have all contributed to the everyday person's awareness of Witchcraft as a viable, modern religious path."*
>
> —Raymond Buckland[1]

On July 19, 2007, I (Dillon) decided to join the masses of Harry Potter fans at the Harry Potter 7 Release Party at my local Barnes & Noble. I knew I'd be up late, so I swung through the Starbucks drive-through for a grande, double-shot, nonfat, no-whip mocha on my way to the bookstore. I hoped to read the book and post some comments online before going to sleep the next day.

At 11 p.m., the sea of people gathered in the parking lot looked like the crowd at a major college football game. I decided to see how a competing bookstore, Books-A-Million, looked with an hour left in the countdown.

The situation in that parking lot forced me to do a double take too. I had never seen so many people at this store! Fortunately, one poor soul abandoned his parking spot long enough for me to claim my answered prayer—finding a parking place within a two-mile radius of the bookstore.

I purchased my book voucher (*only* $20 tonight?) and took my place in line in front of a young mother with an infant and behind a brother and sister dressed in full Harry Potter regalia.

I asked a lot of questions—and listened. Here are some of the comments I heard:

"I've read every book twice. They're amazing!"
  —An adult female

"I've grown up on Harry Potter."
  —A junior high girl

"I never come to the bookstore except for Harry Potter books."
  —The young mother behind me in line

"Any excuse to stay out after midnight!"
  —A teenage guy

"I'm just glad to see so many young people excited to read anything."
  —A parent chilling on a couch while her Hermione-costumed daughter celebrated with her friends

Finally, the clock struck midnight and the line began to surge forward. Once inside the store, I grabbed my copy of the book, tossed my empty coffee cup, and headed for my office to discover the fate of Harry and his friends. By the time the sun was about to rise again, I had read the book and posted some of the first online comments regarding issues parents should be concerned about in the newest Harry Potter tome.

MY CHANCE *to* HELP

Some of my online comments on the seventh and last Harry Potter book were picked up by CNN.com, CBSnews.com, and at least one Harry Potter fan website. I also posted some comments on my personal blog. I adapted the material into an article that became the most requested article of the year for the Christian organization that I serve.[2]

Oh, and according to Scholastic, the final book in the series, *Harry Potter and the Deathly Hallows*, sold an amazing 8.3 million copies in its first 24 hours—a record in the history of book publishing.

But has Pottermania promoted witchcraft? And even if it has, does it really matter? In this chapter, we'll evaluate how the influence of the Harry Potter series and other popular media has contributed to the explosive growth of Wicca and witchcraft. In addition, we'll investigate why we, as consumers of Harry Potter books and other "magickal media" (along with our parents, children, grandparents, and other influencers), should be concerned about our culture's increasing interest in Wicca and paganism.

What Is Harry Potter All About?

For those who have not read the Harry Potter books or watched the films, the Harry Potter saga begins with a young English boy, Harry, who is told he is a wizard. Mistreated by the uncle and aunt who raise him, he enrolls in the Hogwarts School of Witchcraft and Wizardry. There he meets other wizards and witches, including Ron Weasley, Hermione Granger, a student bully named Draco, the headmaster Dumbledore, a half-giant named Hagrid, and the ultimate bad guy, the one-who-must-not-be-named, Voldemort.

The series consists of seven young adult novels, published beginning in 1997 by J.K. Rowling, a rags-to-riches author who is now considered to be the wealthiest person in the UK. Here are the titles of the seven books and the dates of their releases:

Harry Potter and the Sorcerer's Stone	1997
Harry Potter and the Chamber of Secrets	1998
Harry Potter and the Prisoner of Azkaban	1999
Harry Potter and the Goblet of Fire	2000
Harry Potter and the Order of the Phoenix	2003
Harry Potter and the Half-Blood Prince	2005
Harry Potter and the Deathly Hallows	2007

The films based on the books have been some of the top-grossing films in the U.S. For instance, the first film adaptation, released in 2001, raked in over $976 million worldwide and received three Academy Award nominations.[3] The sixth film, *The Half-Blood Prince*, is scheduled for a November 2008 release, with the final film, *The Deathly Hallows*, slated for 2010. In the end, the impact of these books will have extended over a 13-year period, influencing the culture of an entire generation.

Why Should I Be Concerned About Harry Potter?

The seventh and final book in the series, *Harry Potter and the Deathly Hallows*, is marketed as "safe for youth to read." But is it?

Let's take a look at the content of this seventh book as a representation of what we find in the series as a whole. In my review, I observed several key points of concern: vulgar language, a high level of violence, and disturbing spiritual content.

Vulgar Language

When I read *Harry Potter and the Deathly Hallows*, I was shocked to discover how much vulgarity was included. The following list gives you some idea of the level of mature language used in the book:

- "'And are they getting married in my bedroom?' asked Ron furiously. 'No! So why in the name of Merlin's saggy left—'" (page 92). The text ends there, but the words lead the reader to fill in the blank.

- "snogging" (page 116). According to thefreedictionary.com, this means, "affectionate play (or foreplay without contact with the genital organs)." This could be the American equivalent of "making out," but I wouldn't let my kids run around saying the word.

- "How the ruddy h——?" (page 162).

- "d——n" (this word occurs three times: pages 162, 362, and 374).

- "bloody fools" (page 558). A British vulgarity, though probably not considered so by most American readers.

- "bast——d" (page 564).

- "h——l" (page 622).
- "b——h" (page 737).

At least six of these words are considered coarse or vulgar in the American English vocabulary. When I posted my concerns about this on the fan website Potterwatch.com, the webmaster responded, in part,

> The language is accurate. However, the sentiment is mis-directed. I spend time in elementary schools with kids and I know for a fact that they use far more coarse language than is found in the book.
>
> In my personal opinion, which as the site owner I get to interject as I feel fit, the language in the novel is appropri-ate to its reading level, which according to the publisher is "young adult."
>
> Note: Young adult, not Child. So yes, if you're giving this to your child you may want to consider the language. If it's for your teen/young adult then you can feel comfortable that the language is nothing which will "harm their fragile psyches."[4]

According to this explanation, this language is fine to include in reading material for young adults because elementary school kids already use language more coarse than this. But what kind of logic is that? Should we say that it's okay for children to view por-nography because there are some elementary school children who already do? Likewise, we would never suggest that it's acceptable to promote marijuana usage among children just because some kids already use it.

It all comes back to the question, "What's your standard for evaluation?" If your desire as a parent is for your child to fill his or her mind with healthy content that helps them grow into people of integrity, you need to know what your children are reading. You *do* have a say regarding what is acceptable and what is not.

A High Level of Violence

If *Harry Potter and the Deathly Hallows* were made into a movie, the rating would be PG-13, just as it was for *Harry Potter and the Order of the Phoenix*. Why this rating for a movie with coarse language, violence, and some really scary scenes? According to the Motion Picture Association of America, "There may be depictions of violence in a PG-13 movie, but generally not both realistic and extreme or persistent violence."[5] However, *The Deathly Hallows* does contain scenes of realistic, extreme, and persistent violence.

For example, after the death of the character Mad-Eye Moody early in the story, his friends are unable to find his body. Later, however, Harry discovers Mad-Eye's eyeball on the front of someone's door, where it is being used as a security measure. Harry steals the eye and later buries it at the base of an old tree as a measure of respect.

Another disturbing scene occurs when Voldemort puts the "sorting hat" on the student Neville's head and sets it on fire during the battle of Hogwarts. Fortunately, reinforcements arrive and the battle begins again. Neville escapes and chops off the head of Nagini the snake, which contains part of Voldemort's soul.

BLOOD ON *the* GROUND

Because of its repeated violence, some could even argue that if *The Deathly Hallows* is made into a film, it should be R-rated. In total, 76 characters are killed. That's nearly one person per every ten pages of the book (in all fairness, 54 of these occur in one battle, the Battle of Hogwarts). In addition, Harry himself dies and comes back to life after a brief discussion with Dumbledore.

The only romantic content of the book is a kiss shared between Harry and Ginny, but the violence is more graphic than in any previous title in the Potter series.

Disturbing Spiritual Content

The spiritual content presents by far the most disturbing, yet intriguing, aspect of the final Harry Potter tale. Two specific New Testament verses are quoted as part of the storyline. First, when Harry goes to find his parents' graves, he finds the tomb of Kendra Dumbledore engraved with the words, "Where your treasure is, there is your heart." This quote echoes Matthew 6:21 and Luke 12:34. In the same chapter (page 328), Harry finds the tombstone of his parents, bearing this inscription: "The last enemy that shall be destroyed is death." These words were originally written by the apostle Paul in 1 Corinthians 15:26.

Another spiritual theme apparent in the storyline deals with the resurrection stone, one of three objects that are considered part of the Deathly Hallows. This stone allows the user to see and communicate with the dead. Harry uses it once to speak with his dead parents, his godfather Sirius Black, and a character named Remus Lupin. He later loses the stone in the Forbidden Forest, where it remains at the end of the story.

Toward the end of the book, Harry realizes he must allow Voldemort to kill him in order for Voldemort to die. Why? Because part of the dark wizard's soul lives *in* Harry. He allows himself to be killed by the *Avada Kedavra* curse, after which Harry awakens in the afterlife (or a dream?) and speaks with his headmaster, Dumbledore. Though it is never completely clear whether Harry dies or not, his return causes onlookers to shout, "He's alive!" This brings to mind the disciples' response to Christ's resurrection. After Harry "comes back to life," he returns and helps finish off Voldemort to win the battle of Hogwarts.

The disturbing witchcraft-related spiritual themes from the other books in the Potter series continue in the last book as well. The characters use their wands to shoot spells back and forth in battle, using phrases that often date back to actual ancient curses. Remember the *Avada Kedavra* mentioned above? In an interview, author J.K. Rowling made the following comments:

Its origin is an ancient spell in Aramaic, and it is the original of *abracadabra,* which means "let the thing be destroyed." Originally, it was used to cure illness and the "thing" was the illness, but I decided to make it the "thing" as in the person standing in front of me. I take a lot of liberties with things like that. I twist them round and make them mine.[6]

Another major spiritual theme relates to objects called *horcruxes.* A horcrux, according to the Potter series, is a receptacle in which a dark wizard has hidden a part of his soul for the purpose of attaining immortality. This is a fictional idea, but one associated with the dark arts (dark magic) in the series. Voldemort has divided his soul into seven parts in order to obtain immortality as part of his desire to overtake the wizarding world.

We also read several times about *occulmency.* (This term surfaces in the book at points when Harry's scar is hurting.) According to the Harry Potter Lexicon, occulmency is "the art of magically defending the mind against external penetration, sealing it against magical intrusion and influence."[7] As applied in *The Deathly Hallows,* Harry can "see" Voldemort's actions in his mind. A mental battle rages, with descriptions that are similar to instances of demonic possession recorded in the Bible.

Dementors—soul-sucking, ghostlike figures who protect the prison of Azkaban—also appear again, resembling demons in description. In addition, Harry meets a woman named Bathilda Bagshot, who he thinks is a friend, but soon finds out is simply a trap. Bathilda's body is actually inhabited and controlled by Voldemort's snake, Nagini.

Evaluating Pottermania

J.K. Rowling has crafted an imaginative, creative, and well-told story. On the surface, her goal does not seem to be to recruit anyone into witchcraft. However, the content of *Harry Potter and the Deathly Hallows,* representative of the other Harry Potter books and films, should concern parents. Probably the issue of greatest concern is the nonbiblical spiritual content that glorifies witchcraft, spell casting, potion making, astrology, numerology, interaction with the dead, and other dark supernatural practices, suggesting these are innocent and harmless activities.

The Bible clearly states that those who desire to obey God should avoid all forms of witchcraft and sorcery. When God gave His people the Law, He said, "Let no one be found among you who sacrifices his son or daughter in the fire, who practices divination or sorcery, interprets omens, engages in witchcraft, or casts spells, or who is a medium or spiritist or who consults the dead" (Deuteronomy 18:10-11).

Rather than considering witchcraft to be harmless, parents must realize the Bible's position toward it. The apostle John wrote, "Do not imitate what is evil but what is good" (3 John 11). A word of caution for parents: Ultimately, *you* are the gatekeepers of what enters your home and your child's life. And guarding your children's hearts is no easy task.

Michael O'Brien writes in *A Landscape with Dragons*,

> If a child's reading is habitually in the area of the super-natural, is there not a risk that he will develop an insatiable appetite for it, an appetite that grows ever stronger as it is fed? Will he be able to recognize the boundaries between spiritually sound imaginative works and the deceptive ones? Here is another key point for parents to consider: Are we committed to discussing these issues with our children? Are we willing to accompany them, year after year, as their tastes develop, advising caution here, sanctioning liberality there, each of us, young and old, learning as we go?...Are we willing to sacrifice precious time to pre-read some novels about which we may have doubts? Are we willing to invest effort to help our children choose the right kind of fantasy literature from libraries and bookstores?[8]

As Christian parents, we should monitor our children's involvement with Harry Potter and related materials. Further, we must be aware that this series and similar books and films are not just media that kids will consume and then forget about. This type of entertainment can have a profound influence on children's language, actions, and beliefs.

For parents, here are some simple ways to gauge the appropriateness of the material your kids are reading and watching.

1. Read up on the spiritual background of controversial books, films, or video games.[9]

2. Pre-read portions of books and review films you have genuine concerns about.

3. Provide clear guidelines to your children and teenagers regarding what types of reading material and other media are acceptable for your family.

4. Set an example of personal Bible reading and the reading of other healthy materials as a model for your children.

George Barna adds a point that is also important to consider:

> The Bible notes that believers should always be ready to answer questions about their faith whenever people ask. While not minimizing the spiritual danger of stories like Harry Potter, the upside of such content is that it raises questions of purpose, destiny, relationships, isolation, redemption, spiritual power and more—the very topics that are so important to the message of Christianity. But, as things stand, many parents and church leaders are letting those spiritual opportunities go to waste.[10]

Principles of witchcraft provide the backdrop for many aspects of the Harry Potter series, but there is much more to its history. In our next chapter, we'll explore the origins of witchcraft, and Wicca in particular. Is Wicca really an ancient religion that predates

Christianity and then was revived in the last generation? Or is it a relatively new belief system?

Keep reading as we continue our discussion of the (new) old ways of Wicca.

The (New) Old Ways

Wicca's Past

"Salem is to Wiccans what Golgotha is to Christians."
—JESSICA[1]

As the first rays of summer sunlight began to spill over the village of Salem, Massachusetts, a procession of dark figures made its way toward Gallows Hill. Five empty nooses hung from a wooden frame, swaying in the early morning breeze.

Village leaders marched five women accused of witchcraft—Rebecca Nurse, Sarah Good, Elizabeth How, Sarah Wild, and Susanna Martin—up the hill to be hanged. One of Salem's ministers, Reverend Noyes, made a final appeal to the women "to save their immortal souls by confessing their practice of witchcraft." But they continued to plead their innocence. Sadly, these five so-called "witches" were executed on that fateful day of July 19, 1692. Afterward, their bodies were taken down and placed in a shallow grave.[2]

Witchcraft—and negative attitudes toward it—have a long and storied history in America. In Massachusetts in the late 1600s, false accusations and hysteria caused the death of many women and men, most of whom had nothing to do with witchcraft at all.

But how do our country's early brushes with witchcraft tie in with the popularity of Wicca? And how did this religion grow from a minuscule beginning into a giant phenomenon that works its magick so openly across our nation's religious landscape? To answer these questions and more, let's examine Wicca's beginnings.

Wicca: An Old or a New Religion?

Scott Cunningham, author of over 30 books on witchcraft, defines Wicca as "a loosely organized Pagan religion centering around reverence for the creative forces of Nature, usually symbolized by a goddess and a god."[3] That tells us what Wicca is, but when did this religion develop, and why?

If you ask Wiccans whether theirs is an old or a new religion, most will say "old." Laurie Cabot, one of America's most prominent witches, told a reporter that "Wicca is pre-Christian, an Earth religion. There are two supremes, a god and a goddess. It's an art, a science, and a religion."[4]

Like Cabot, many Wiccan practitioners believe that their craft stems from a religious system thousands of years old. But we'll find that this is not the case.

MAGIC *and* MAGICK

"Is magick with a *k* different from magic? You bet. Both words come from the same root, meaning 'to be able, to have power,' but magic is what an entertainer does on stage—creating illusions, performing card tricks, making quarters disappear, sawing a hapless volunteer in half. Magick falls within the realm of witchcraft and may include spells, healing, the harnessing of psychic forces, and even divination."[5]

The native people groups of every country, from Afghanistan to Zimbabwe, have had, at some point, their own pagan religious practices. For example, in Ireland, priests called Druids became the ancient Celtic spiritual leaders. And in Scandinavia, Norse gods and goddesses were created to explain different aspects of nature.[6]

✦ Wicca, however, is not an ancient, indigenous religious practice unique to any people group. Rather, it's a very recent, twentieth-century religion created by melding ancient traditions with principles of modern psychology, mythology, mysticism, magick, and pagan spirituality. Phyllis Curott, a Wiccan high priestess who serves as one of the most prominent pagan religious leaders in the United States, describes Wicca as "an amalgamation of free-masonry, mythology, folk practices, nineteenth-century American pantheism, transcendentalism, feminism, spiritualism, Buddhism, and shamanism."[7] That's quite a combo!

Silver RavenWolf writes,

> Wicca, as you practice the religion today, is a new religion, barely fifty years old. The techniques you use at present are not entirely what your elders practiced even thirty years ago. Of course, threads of "what was" weave through the tapestry of "what is now."…In no way can we replicate to perfection the precise circumstances of environment, society, culture, religion and magick a hundred years ago, or a thousand. Why would we want to? The idea is to go forward with the knowledge of the past, tempered by the tools of our own age.[8]

How Did Wicca Begin?

Gerald Gardner, a retired British civil servant, developed the major tenets of the Wiccan belief system in the mid-twentieth century. Gardner became deeply interested in witchcraft and the occult and reportedly joined a coven in England in 1938. As he became more involved with witchcraft, he began to develop a religion that he called *Wica* (with one *c*). Later, the religion was referred to as *Wicca*.

Gardner wrote fictional stories as a means of sharing his beliefs about witchcraft and this new religious system he had developed. One of his most famous stories, "High Magic's Aid," was published in 1949. Gardner later wrote a nonfiction account of his experiences with witchcraft called *Witchcraft Today*, which was published in 1954.[9]

Despite the recent history of Wicca, many Wiccans continue to believe and teach that Wicca is an "ancient" or "pre-Christian" religion. Author Steve Russo says this on the subject:

Some say Wicca is a direct religious movement of the ancient Druids and Celts. Others claim it is much more modern—having been started within the last fifty or sixty years. Still other people believe it's at least twenty-five thousand years old. Starhawk, author of the book *The Spiral Dance: A Rebirth of the Ancient Religion of the Goddess*, thinks that witchcraft had its beginnings close to thirty-five thousand years ago.[10]

One Wiccan writes,

Wicca is...based upon the reconstruction of pre-Christian traditions originating in Ireland, Scotland, and Wales. While much of the information of how our ancestors lived, worshiped and believed has been lost due to the efforts of the medieval church to wipe our existence from history, we try to reconstruct those beliefs to the best of our ability...

Thanks to archaeological discoveries, we now have basis to believe that the origins of our belief system can be traced even further back to the Paleolithic peoples who worshipped a Hunter God and a Fertility Goddess. With the discovery of these cave paintings, estimated to be around 30,000 years old, depicting a man with the head of a stag, and a pregnant woman standing in a circle with eleven other people, it can reasonably be assumed that Witchcraft is one of the oldest belief systems known in the world today. These archetypes are clearly recognized by Wiccans...and predate Christianity by roughly 28,000 years, making [Christianity] a mere toddler in the spectrum of time as we know it.[11]

Though many well-meaning people believe that Wicca is ancient, as we've already noted, this is simply not the case. Wicca does borrow some traditions and rites from ancient religions, but the actual Wiccan belief system itself is less than 100 years old and represents a very recent development on the continuum of religious history. The cave paintings referred to in the preceding quote may depict early pagan worship customs, but they are unrelated to modern Wicca.

ACKNOWLEDGING HISTORY

Interestingly, one of Wicca's primary teaching websites (www.wicca .org) clearly states that Wicca is a recently developed religion, though it suggests that Wicca started in the early nineteenth century rather than in the twentieth.[12]

When Did Wicca Become an Official Religion?

In 1986, "The Church of Wicca" was officially declared a religion by a U.S. Federal Appeals Court in the case of *Dettmer vs. Landon*. Wiccan holidays and practices now have legal protection in the U.S. and many other countries. Most universities allow Wiccan students to miss classes to observe pagan holidays in the same way that Christians take time off to celebrate Christmas and Easter.

An article titled "Wicca's World: Looking into the Pagan Phenomenon" in the ZENIT Daily Dispatch (an international news agency with roots in the Catholic Church) reveals some of the ways in which pagan practices are becoming more widespread—and the legal rights and protections that Wiccans are receiving.

First, a Dutch court ruled that the costs of witchcraft lessons can be tax-deductible. The Leeuwarden District Court confirmed that people have the legal right to write off the costs of schooling— including training in witchcraft. At the time of the article's release, Margarita Rongen, who runs the "Witches' Homestead" in Holland, charged over $2600 for a full witchcraft course. Rongen has trained hundreds of disciples over the past four decades. Witchcraft courses and schools have popped up all over the country, and now their fees are tax-deductible.

In addition, prisons in England are hiring pagan priests and chaplains to give spiritual advice to inmates who have converted to paganism. According to prison rules, these prisoners are allowed a chaplain in the same way as Christians or those of other faiths. Pagan priests may use wine and wands in their in-prison ceremonies. Pagan inmates may keep a hoodless robe, incense, and a piece of religious jewelry among their personal possessions. They also have permission to pray, chant, perform pagan rituals, and read religious texts in their cells. All prison administrators were given complete guides to paganism, based on information supplied by the Pagan Federation.[13]

As this article indicates, in prisons, schools, businesses, the military, and many other organizations, Wicca and its followers now receive the same rights and protections as followers of Christianity, Judaism, Islam, and other world religions.

Where Did the Term *Wicca* Come From?

Gerald Gardner claimed to have heard the word *Wicca* from other practitioners during his experiences in his coven in the woods of England:

> I was half-initiated before the word "Wica" which they used hit me like a thunderbolt, and I knew where I was, and that the Old Religion still existed. And so I found myself in the Circle, and there took the usual oath of secrecy, which bound me not to reveal certain things…

> ⭐As they (the Dane and Saxon invaders of England) had no witches of their own, they had no special name for them; however, they made one up from *wig* ("an idol"), and *laer* ("learning"): *wiglaer*, which they shortened into 'Wicca.'[14]

In her book *The Rebirth of Witchcraft*, Wiccan author and high priestess Doreen Valiente suggests an alternative—that *Wicca* comes from the Indo-European root *weik*, which relates to things connected with magick and religion.[15]

Other sources suggest that both *witch* and *Wicca* come from the German root *wic*, meaning "to bend or to turn."⭐Witches were believed to have the ability to change or "bend" natural events using magic.[16]

Why Do People Choose Wicca?

The Cafeteria Appeal

Many people love Wicca for its cafeteria-style spirituality—it allows its followers to pick and choose what they want to believe. Anne Niven, editor in chief of *newWitch* magazine, told an MSNBC interviewer, "If you ask three witches to describe their beliefs, you'll probably get about four answers."[17]

In addition, Wicca is personal and adaptable. Wiccans can worship privately as solitary practitioners of the craft, or they may join a coven. They can create their own brand of Wicca that works for them. One Wiccan writes, "Really, there's no one true or right way to practice the craft. Wicca is what you make of it."[18]

I (Marla) interviewed a teen named Jessica—a soft-spoken, articulate girl who wears a pentacle and observes the craft. When I asked her why she chose to follow Wicca, she said, "Wicca gives me room to breathe. It's malleable. When I practice it, I feel free. But Christianity seems so rigid. My parental units tell me, 'If you don't do things exactly the way the Bible says, you're going to hell.'" She smiled ruefully, but her pain was evident. "I'm surrounded by spastic Christians," she said. Jessica still lives at home with her Christian parents. They know she practices Wicca, but they encourage her to remain faithful to her spiritual roots.

"How did Wicca get started as a religion?" I asked Jessica next.

"Wicca itself is a new religion, but it's based on ancient religions that have been around since the beginning of civilization. For example, some of the trees that we hold in high regard, such as oak and willow, have been worshiped for centuries. Basically, Wicca is a modernized druidic religion."

"What about the witches in Salem?" I asked.

"I don't think they were really witches at all," she said. "But I guess you could say that Salem is to Wiccans what Golgotha is to Christians. Visiting Salem is a way to open our eyes to [the persecution] that we really face as witches.

"Most of the people who go to Salem go because they really want to explore the history and roots of Wicca. A friend of mine went, but she got really deeply into black magic while she was there." Jessica's face clouded for a moment, and she looked down. After a pause, she said quietly, "She was killed in a car wreck on the way home."[19]

I expressed my sadness for Jessica's loss. At the end of the interview, I complimented her on her ability to share her experiences so openly and articulate her faith so well.

"The younger you are, the easier it is to learn new things," she stated simply.

Her stories made me aware of the struggle many Wiccans experience daily.

The Community Appeal

Many Wiccans use books and the internet for help and to gain greater knowledge in practicing their craft. The internet boasts millions of websites that provide Wiccans with information, doctrine, spells, encouragement—and a sense of community.

From its beginnings, Wicca has been labeled an *occult* ("hidden") religion. Many of its adherents have felt persecuted for their beliefs and lifestyles. As a result, they band together to support one another. Many young people have chosen to follow Wicca because of this sense of community. Others enjoy the earth-centered aspects of the religion. Some teens join Wicca as a means of rebelling against their parents, protesting the status quo, or because they do not feel accepted among their peers at school or in their youth group at church.

The Witches' Voice (www.witchvox.com) is one of today's most popular Wiccan websites, offering thousands of articles by Wiccan practitioners. On this site, a Wiccan named Luna Morgan writes about her beliefs and the rituals she practices:

> As a Pagan American, I am so blessed. Every full moon and on the Sabbats, I attend circle with hundreds of other Pagans in my community. Most of my neighborhood is Pagan, and I

know that my kids play with kids who grew up the same way. I think we have a few Christians at the end of the block, but they don't make a big deal about what they practice or try to convert anybody. I'm sure that what is said about them isn't true; they seem like such nice people. The United States of America has laws that protect us from theocracy and everyone is free to practice their own religion in peace.[20]

Morgan uses some of the same terminology to refer to Christians that Christians often use to refer to Wiccans! While I (Marla) do not agree with all of her views, I appreciate Morgan's point that Wiccans want what most people desire—the ability to practice their faith in peace without facing condemnation from others. The words and actions that Christians often use to "show care" or "provide accountability" may just feel like persecution to a person of a pagan faith.

Wiccans, like all people, want to be loved; they want to belong. They desire beauty, wonder, magic, and power. They want to have control over their lives and their destiny. I have found many of them to be sensitive, kindhearted people who seek to worship "the God and the Goddess," to love the earth, to protect the environment, and to improve and enhance their lives through magick.

Like many of us, Wiccans believe that their hearts and souls have been starved by technology and the lack of meaningful relationships with God, other people, and nature. Many people turn to Wicca because they long for a faith that feels real and tangible. Often, they're seeking a powerful spiritual and emotional experience, and they don't receive that in their personal worship or at their local church.

A LONGING *for* WONDER

Donald Miller, author of *Blue Like Jazz*, comments on the human condition: "Ravi Zacharias says that the heart desires wonder and magic. He says technology is what man uses to supplant the desire for wonder...What the heart is really longing to do is worship, to stand in awe of a God we don't understand and can't explain."[21]

Tim Baker, author of *Dewitched*, writes,

> Humans are interesting creatures. We have the chance
> to surrender our lives to a Loving Creator who knows us
> and wants the best for us. Humans, however, choose to do
> everything they can to stay in control of their lives. Believing
> that we can do a better job and thinking that we're better
> equipped to handle our lives, we will ignore the existence
> of God. We will do our best to stay in control of ourselves
> and keep God on the outskirts of our lives.[22]

The apostle Paul, author of several New Testament books, understood the tension between people's desire for God and their desire to
be the rulers of their own lives. A well-trained religious and political scholar, Paul investigated the claims and belief systems of the
religious and pagan leaders of his day. He wanted to be able to understand what they believed so he could share with them the good news
that they could trust God with their lives and live in eternity with
Him. Understanding their experiences, beliefs, and desires enabled
Paul to effectively communicate the gospel to them.

We chose to do the same with Wicca—and so can you, now that
you're informed about how and when Wicca began and how the
movement has grown.

In our next chapter, we'll learn more about Wicca's teachings.
We'll glean spiritual truths and practical principles that will help you
get a better grasp of your own beliefs and learn to share them with
pagans in a simple, effective way.

The Book of Shadows

Wicca's Teachings

"Jesus' command to preach the gospel and make disciples of all nations invariably includes witches. In order to do so, it is necessary that we understand who they are and what they believe."

—RICHARD HOWE[1]

Last fall, I (Dillon) observed local Halloween traditions in six states across the U.S.—Tennessee, Georgia, North Carolina, Texas, Indiana, and Michigan. Here are some of my findings:

Common to All States

+ Halloween superstores.

+ Lots of candy (I ate more than my share!).

+ Schools and businesses celebrating and sometimes even closing for Halloween.

+ Homes decorated with lights, inflatables, and pumpkins.

+ Costume parties in clubs, bars, schools, churches, offices—everywhere!

+ Did I mention *lots* of candy?

Different from State to State

+ An attraction at Lookout Mountain near Chattanooga featured a maze cut out of a field of corn.

+ Stoney Creek Farms in suburban Indianapolis celebrated the harvest with a pick-your-own-pumpkin patch, rides, and hayrides.

+ Atlanta offered a "Boo at the Zoo" celebration with a costume contest, fortune-telling, and much more.

+ Several churches in Grand Rapids held Halloween alternative parties. The area also hosted several "haunted woods" opportunities, including a "Haunted Iell" that took people through an abandoned mine shaft and scary caves.

Candy, costumes, and parties I expected. Fortune-telling at the zoo I did not. Of course, having the day off from work on Halloween would be great. But I was concerned by the subtly dangerous influence I saw in every state I visited.

The spiritual trend I discovered is, *witchcraft is no longer taboo.* In reality, this trend has been growing for a number of years. A person dressed as a witch or sorcerer doesn't bother most people anymore. Those who are a part of "generation hex" accept witchcraft as just another thing people do.

But anyone who has investigated the beliefs of Wicca knows that the idea that "witchcraft is harmless" simply isn't true. In this chapter, we'll share some of Wicca's core beliefs. As we do, we'll discover the ways some of these beliefs are at odds with a biblical worldview.

Common Misconceptions About Wicca

Wicca and its participants often are cast in a negative and inaccurate light. Though Wiccan beliefs differ significantly from biblical ones, Wiccans...

+ do not worship Satan (in fact, they don't believe he even exists).
+ do not sacrifice virgins or infants.
+ do not have a single, authoritative Witches' Bible or other Bible-like book.
+ do not fly on brooms.
+ are not trying to convert you or your children to Wicca.
+ do not have a conspiracy to destroy the church, shut down the public education system, or create a single world government.

But if Wiccans are not walking around wearing pointy black hats and casting evil spells on people who follow God, what *are* they doing? And what do they believe?

Wiccan Ways

As we mentioned in chapter 1, the foundational creed of Wicca is, "An ye harm none, do as ye will"—if what you do doesn't hurt anyone else, then do whatever you want.

This sounds great, but in reality this statement doesn't make sense. How do I know for certain that what I am doing isn't hurting someone else? And what if I *think* my actions are not hurting someone, but they actually are? For instance, if I chose to drink alcohol excessively, I could argue that it would be hurting only me. However, the reality is that such a habit also would hurt my wife, my children, and others around me. And if I always just do want I want, that's selfish. Being a loving person and a part of a healthy society requires me to sometimes sacrifice what I want to do for the sake of serving God and others. (In fact, there is great joy in that sacrifice.)

✡The Wiccan creed above (also known as the Wiccan Rede) provides no standard for determining what is right or wrong other than personal preference and choice.

In addition to the Wiccan Rede, Wicca offers a few other consistently held beliefs. Some statements that help form the basis for Wiccan values are the Wiccan Law, the Rule of Three, the Wiccan Code of Chivalry, and the Principles of Wiccan Belief.

THE WICCAN LAW

Bide the Wiccan Law ye must,
In perfect love and perfect trust.
These eight words the Wiccan Rede fulfill,
An ye harm none do as ye will.
And ever mind the Rule of Three,
What ye send out comes back to thee.
Follow this with mind and heart.
And merry ye meet and merry ye part.

Several versions of this Law exist, though this shortened version has been commonly used throughout Wiccan literature. All versions of the Wiccan Law contain both the Wiccan Rede and the Rule of Three.

The Rule of Three

The Rule of Three states that "what ye send out comes back to thee." This rule is used in reference to both good and bad deeds or spells, meaning that what you do to others, whether good or bad, will be returned to you threefold.[2]

This belief brings to mind the Eastern religious concept of *karma*, in which a person's good deeds are returned to them in positive ways, and their negative acts cause them to experience pain, harm, or other negative effects. However, the Rule of Three is not the same as the biblical principle to "do to others what you would have them do to you" (Matthew 7:12, also known as the Golden Rule). Jesus' command is about showing love to others without expecting anything in return. The Rule of Three suggests a built-in return on investment for those who treat others well, and harm for those who do not.

The Wiccan Code of Chivalry

The Wiccan Code of Chivalry (also called the Old Code) is described this way: "That code, as we envision it today, exemplifies a deep love of the Wiccan religion and of those who practice that religion. It is carried forth in some of the wording of an initiation wherein the initiate swears to defend the Lord and Lady and all those who love Them, in this life and all those sure to follow."[3]

Wiccan writings emphasize the importance of helping those in need and standing up for those less fortunate. If a Wiccan believes that what he or she does returns to him or her threefold, that person will be dedicated to doing good to others. Good deeds don't just benefit other people; they help to better the individual's own life by sending out positive energy into the universe that will return even stronger.

The Principles of Wiccan Belief

Wicca also draws heavily on a list of beliefs developed in 1974 by the Council of American Witches.[4] The "Principles of Wiccan Belief" include...

1. Know yourself.

2. Know your Craft.

3. Learn.

4. Apply knowledge with wisdom.

5. Achieve balance.

6. Keep your words in good order.

7. Keep your thoughts in good order.

8. Celebrate life.

9. Attune with the cycle of the earth.

10. Breathe and eat correctly.

11. Exercise the body.

12. Meditate.

13. Honor the Goddess and the God.[5]

Notice that many of these principles correlate with beliefs and teachings of Christianity. However, some clearly are at odds with what the Bible teaches. Of greatest concern is number 13 (more about "the Goddess and the God" later). Christians would not be able to hold or endorse this belief because they serve only one God as revealed through Jesus Christ (John 14:6).

Other Beliefs

Most Wiccans feel disappointed, frustrated, and angry about the stereotypes and misconceptions outsiders have of them. In our research, we've found that, contrary to popular belief,

+ *Wiccans are not Satan worshipers.* As we mentioned a few pages earlier, Wiccans honor the Goddess and the God and revere the earth. Most Wiccans don't believe in the existence of Satan.

+ *Wiccans do not cast evil spells (or at least they're not supposed to).*

Because of the Law of Three and the Rede, Wiccans believe there is no advantage to casting evil or negative spells on others.

+ *Wiccans are not all female.* About two-thirds of Wiccans are female. But many of the men involved are very influential, and some of the most popular Wiccan teachers and writers of our time are male.

The other difficulty in evaluating Wiccan beliefs is that very few beliefs are consistently held by all. While we will compare Wiccan and biblical theology later in this book, we've listed some of Wicca's core beliefs below as a quick reference guide:[6]

+ *God.* Contemporary Wiccans worship the Great Mother Goddess and her partner, the Horned God (also called Gaius or Pan), but these and a host of other pagan deities are said to represent various aspects of an impersonal creative force called "The One" or "The All"—reflecting the current influence of Eastern monism popularized in New Age thought. Wiccans regard all aspects of nature—plants, rocks, planets—as having spirit. This stands in clear contrast with the biblical concept of one God who is creator of all.

+ *Jesus.* Some Wiccans view Jesus as an enlightened person or a wizard, not the Son of God born of a virgin. Most believe that he was Gaius or a great prophet or religious leader, but that's all. Jesus may be viewed positively by some Wiccans, but his personality, attributes, and actions are redefined by Wiccans in a way that contrasts sharply with the Jesus we know from the Bible.

+ *The Holy Spirit.* Wiccans believe it matters little whether we associate with the divine as the "Father, Son, and Holy Ghost" or "The One—Goddess and God." Ultimately, the concept is the same, according to Wiccan writings. Wiccans rarely mention the Holy Spirit. When they do, they usually assert that

He is just one of many spirits rather than a unique person of the Trinitarian God as taught in biblical Christianity.

+ *The Bible.* Wiccans may believe that the Bible is an important book, but they perceive it as one of many ways to find enlightenment rather than considering it to be the authoritative source of God's truth.

+ *Sin.* Wiccans believe that any action is acceptable as long as no one gets hurt by it. As a result, sin is redefined as acts that hurt others rather than offenses toward a holy God. According to the organization Magic Wicca, "In Wicca, we do not have a specific concept of sin."[7]

+ *Salvation.* Wiccans believe that all religions lead to the same destination; they simply use different paths to get there. All people should therefore be free to choose their own path.[8] "Many paths to God" may sound like a good idea, but it's the opposite of Jesus' teaching that He is "*the* way and *the* truth and *the* life" (John 14:6) and that there is only one name by which we can be saved—the name of Jesus Christ (Acts 4:12).

+ *Angels.* Most Wiccans do not believe in the biblical view of angels, but rather in beings called "the Watchers." Raven Grimassi describes them as "an ancient race who have evolved beyond the need for physical form."[9]

+ *The afterlife.* Wiccans believe that after they experience life to its fullest and come to know and understand every aspect and emotion of life (usually after many reincarnations), their deity will let them into the Summerland. The Summerland also functions as a place of rest between incarnations. As the name entails, the Summerland is a place of beauty and peace, where everything people hold close to their hearts is preserved in its fullest beauty for eternity.[10] The concept of hell or eternal retribution taught in the Bible is considered offensive and false by most Wiccans.

JOINING WICCA

Scott Cunningham writes, "Wicca doesn't seek new members. This has been a major stumbling block to those wishing to learn its rites and ways of magic. Wicca doesn't solicit because, unlike most western religions, it doesn't claim to be the one true way to deity."[11]

Now What?

Recently, I (Dillon) was interviewed about other religions for a Christian radio show. After I shared some information on Wicca, the questions from my interviewer became more pointed and defensive. I've noticed the same response from many other church leaders and parents. They have good intentions, but their reaction jumps to "threat status orange" every time a witchcraft-related issue arises.

On one hand, we're responsible for evaluating the spiritual ideas and philosophies that come our way. That's what this book is all about. However, many Wiccans have highly critical attitudes toward Christians and Christianity, and for good reason—many of them have been deeply hurt by "well-meaning Christians." What if, instead of bashing those involved in witchcraft, we showed genuine concern for them as a starting point for meaningful dialogue?

Last Halloween we sent the following e-mail to our friends and family:

We LOVE witches!

Really, we do...and so does God.

This is a personal invitation to *help start a movement*—to take the one day when witchcraft is most highlighted in our culture and use it to **pray for those involved in witchcraft to experience Christ's love.**

So say YES! Please take a moment out of your busy day *right now* to pray for those involved in witchcraft on Halloween.

For far too long, Christians have sinned by *failing to show genuine concern* for those involved in witchcraft. Witches and Wiccans are people like the rest of us, with deep spiritual needs—and part of a rapidly growing spiritual movement in our culture.

Did you know that Wicca (the most popular form of modern witchcraft) is the fastest-growing religion in America? At its current rate, **Wicca could be the second-largest religion in America by 2012. That's only five years away!** *Now* is the time to pray.

Here's how it works:

1. *Pray right now* for those in your community involved in witchcraft.

2. *Forward this e-mail* to anyone who will do the same.

What happened? I offended some Christians when I said we have sinned by failing to show genuine love and concern for those in witchcraft. I offended some Wiccans because I indicated that following the Wiccan belief system is not God's desire for their lives. But those who prayed began to take their concerns for those involved in witchcraft and apply them in a positive way.

The idea for my audacious e-mail began when I was a senior in college at Indiana State University. A few friends said they had heard about some of the activities people from their dorm would be involved in on Halloween night and said we should get together and pray for them.

So we did. On Halloween night from 9 to 11 p.m. (the best time to meet in college), a small group of us joined together to pray for God's safety and intervention in the lives of those who would be in harm's way that night. We honored God by singing songs of worship, and we ended our time hanging out as friends and encouraging one another.

The question that struck me that night continues to wrestle within me today: Why couldn't teenagers, college students, and churches do something similar whenever Halloween is observed?

I extend this invitation to everyone who reads this book, along with anyone who will join us online. Next Halloween, let's pray for those involved in Wicca or witchcraft to consider the way of Christ as the answer to their spiritual needs. I challenge you to join us and to share how God uses you to show Christ's love to those involved in Wicca, witchcraft, and other alternative religions.

The Wide, Wide World of Wicca

Wicca's Practices

> *"Wicca is an organic religion, one that is evolv-
> ing and emerging as a worldwide faith."*
> —EILEEN HOLLAND[1]

Kaytee is a lot like other 16-year-olds. She struggles at school and at home, but she also hopes to become an actress someday. She's fascinated by the supernatural and is searching for power to make her dreams a reality. Kaytee is also a Wiccan. So are her mother, her father, and her eight-year-old sister. Her parents are first-degree witches, but she's still practicing for initiation.

Kaytee is learning the basics of the cone of power and about the gods and goddesses of the magick circle. Everyone at school knows she's into witchcraft, although most don't understand it. She wants to use her first spell to help her get the part of Peter Pan in the school play. "It's like prayer," she says. "I will project that I will get this part of Peter Pan in the musical, harm me none and for the good of all."[2]

For encouragement and support, many young people like Kaytee log onto Witchvox.com, which offers Wiccans the ability to network with people involved in witchcraft around the world. Since its inception in 1997, Witchvox has featured nearly 37,000 articles—in total, these articles have been viewed over 280 million times. Witchvox also includes a social network similar to MySpace, hosting the personal profiles of over 70,000 individuals and groups (teenagers, adults, military personnel, and so on) involved in witchcraft.

One teenager named Megan told me (Dillon) that she felt more confident in her decision to follow the craft after joining Witchvox and connecting with other people who shared her beliefs. "I don't go around flaunting the fact that I call myself a witch and practice witchcraft, because it's not necessary," she said. Megan finds it easier to talk online with others who share her perspective on the God and the Goddess and other spiritual issues.

What Do Wiccans Do?

In chapter 4, we shared some elements of the Wiccan belief system. But what do Wiccans *do*? How do they put their beliefs into practice?

Wicca's practices usually center around rituals performed in a Sacred Circle. Wiccans gather in these circles to cast spells or share passages from special books. They also join together to celebrate Wicca's major holidays, the Sabbats and the Esbats. We'll discuss these holidays a bit later in this chapter.

Create the Sacred Circle

The Sacred Circle is the place where most Wiccan rituals and magick are practiced. One Wiccan writes, "Most of our ritual workings are done in a special space marked off as a Sacred Circle that is cast in a special way. This circle is purified and designated as a protected space for the practitioners and for whatever deities are invoked during the performance of a rite or ritual."[3]

WICCAN EXPRESSIONS

Some common expressions include "Hail and welcome/farewell," "Blessed be" (sometimes abbreviated online or in text messages as B*B), and the closing, "Merry meet and merry part, and merry meet again."[4]

Even prayer is utilized by Wiccans as a means to discover

answers. One Wiccan author writes, "Prayer is another tool open to the Wiccan. [It can be used] when you're absolutely stuck, when the information can't be found in books, or when [it's] found, confuses you. When you have a real need for assistance, ask for it."[5]

Read from Special Books

The Wiccan faith does not uphold a single, sacred book like the Bible or Qur'an, but it does include the following special books unique to Wicca:

+ *The Mirror Book* is essentially a diary, an account of a person's growth as a witch.[6]

+ *The Book of Shadows* "is your Craft workbook containing your ritual and spellcraft information. It is your working guide to your written invocations, rites, and spells."[7]

+ *Coven Book of Shadows:* "Some covens maintain a Coven Book of Shadows. This Coven Book is usually under the control of the High Priestess, who is responsible for any changes to the contents and for its protection."[8]

In his bestselling book *Living Wicca* (over 200,000 copies sold), Scott Cunningham writes, "Books have always been tools of magic."[9] However, in Wicca, no one book is believed to contain clear revelation from God, in contrast with Christians' belief about the Bible. Instead, each person within Wicca has the authority and autonomy to develop his or her own sacred writings in a journal or a personal Mirror Book or Book of Shadows.

Celebrate the Sabbats and Esbats

Wiccans celebrate a sacred calendar called the Wheel of the Year. They typically mark each full moon (and in some cases new moons) with a ritual called an *Esbat*. They also celebrate eight main holidays, called *Sabbats*. Four of these, the cross-quarter days, are greater festivals: *Samhain*, *Beltane* (or May Eve), *Imbolc*, and *Lammas*. The four lesser festivals are the summer solstice (or *Litha*), the winter solstice (or *Yule*), and the spring and autumn equinoxes, sometimes called *Ostara* and *Mabon*.[10]

Like Jewish Shabbats, Wiccan Sabbats begin at sunset the day before the holiday. Four of the Sabbats, the cross-quarter days, coincide with old Celtic fire festivals and are called by their Celtic names. The other four mark important points on the solar calendar. The eight Sabbats are, in summary,

+ February 2: Imbolc
+ March 21: Ostara (spring equinox)
+ May 1: Beltane
+ June 22: Litha, or Midsummer (summer solstice)
+ August 2: Lughnasadh (sometimes spelled Lughnassadh)
+ September 21: Mabon (autumn equinox)
+ October 31–November 1: Samhain
+ December 21: Yule (winter solstice)

During some years, the actual calendar dates of several of these holidays may differ by a day or two. Magickal work and elaborate rituals typically are performed on the Esbats, which mark the phases of the moon. The most important Esbat occurs on the full moon since Wiccans believe magickal power is especially strong on the night of a full moon. Some groups also recognize Esbats of the new moon and the two quarters.

Of great importance in Wicca and other forms of witchcraft is October 31. That date is considered the beginning of the Wiccan Wheel of the Year and a time when the veil between the natural world and the spirit world is thin. Thus, Wiccans believe that on this date they can more easily communicate with the spirit world.

Until recently, Wiccan celebrations of these lunar holidays were usually secretive:

In the recent past, when there were far fewer members of our religion and public understanding of Pagan faiths was non-existent in this country, Wiccans were usually quiet about their religion. The threat of broken marriages, loss of home, job, and even children was quite real. Wiccans had learned to keep their religious activities wrapped in the shadows. Only the closest of relatives or friends knew what these people did on the nights of the full moon (and the reason why they always asked for the day off after Sabbats).[11]

One notable example of these festivals in practice is the Pagan Spirit Gathering held each summer in southeastern Ohio to celebrate the summer solstice. The 2007 gathering included almost a thousand people. According to attendees,

"This was my first year and I will be back. It was a very spiritual experience for me. I practice solitary Wicca; this was my first time with others of the same beliefs. I loved it."
—Diana

"I was amazed that so many pagans and Wiccans would give up a week of their time to travel to such a remote area. It was like being in a tent city full of pagans."
—Jamie

"This was our first trip to PSG and a wonderful one it was! Our girls loved it too. We plan to attend for many years to come, and as a matter of fact we are already pre-planning our packing list now for 2008!"
—Mike, Heather, Aurora, and Tala[12]

Such festivals and gatherings continue to grow in popularity. Many festivals have expanded to include not only Wiccan practitioners but people from an eclectic array of pagan traditions and spiritualities.

Participate in Handfasting and Handparting Rituals

Wiccan weddings are called handfasting, a ritual in which the couple's clasped hands are tied together by a cord or ribbon (reflective of the phrase "tying the knot"). Divorces are sometimes observed with a handparting, a ritual in which the couple may jump over a broom before parting.[13] Some organizations even provide vows for those planning their own handfasting ceremony.

Some Wiccans also observe a ritual called a *Wiccaning*, similar to a christening for an infant. The Wiccaning's purpose is to present an infant to the Goddess and the God for dedication and protection.

TOOLS *and* INSTRUMENTS USED *in* WICCA

The following are tools commonly used in Wicca rituals: an altar, altar candles, altar cloth, *athame* (a double-edged, dark-handled knife), *besom* (sacred broom), *boline* (herb-harvesting knife), cauldron (to hold fire), chalice, incense and holder, pentacle/pentagram symbol, purifying sage, quarter candles, salt container, sword, wand, and water container.[14]

The Five Elements

One Wiccan writes, "In Wicca we use a system of five elements from which all existence is derived. These elements are Air, Fire, Water, Earth, and Spirit."[15] These five elements are associated with the five points of the pentacle symbol.

THE WICCAN PENTACLE

While the pentagram symbol—the five-pointed star—is not exclusive to Wicca, it is the symbol most commonly associated with Wicca in modern times. When the pentagram is circumscribed—depicted within a circle—with one point up, it is called a pentacle. The inverse pentagram, with two points up, is a symbol of the second-degree initiation rite of traditional Wicca.[16]

Many churched Americans believe the practices of witchcraft and Wicca are secretive and small-scale. But mainstream culture not only recognizes but increasingly highlights the efforts of this large group of new faith practitioners. For example, a Kenmore, New York, newspaper recently shared the following business opening:

> Coffee drinkers who want a little something mystical with their cappuccino need look no further. Coffee & A Spell, a newly-opened coffee shop located at 3100 Delaware Avenue in Kenmore, offers a wide selection of coffee, tea and espresso in front and tarot readings in the back, said owner Onyx Serpentfire.[17]

Similar Wicca-based businesses have opened elsewhere. National Public Radio highlighted the story of the Oh My Goddess coffee shop in Denver as part of a major new spiritual trend in America.[18] A local coffee shop that I (Dillon) visited during a trip to Boulder, Colorado, featured a community bulletin board filled primarily with invites to rituals common among Wiccans, including drum circles, palm readings, and visits to psychics.

Some Observations About What Wiccans Do

We can draw a couple of conclusions based on the previous material. First, *Wicca includes a broad, eclectic variety of beliefs and rituals that may be performed by some Wiccans and not by others.* So when you talk with a pagan about his or her spiritual habits, it would be wise to ask what *he or she* does, rather than assume he or she performs all of the rituals described in this book.

Second, it's clear that *many of these rituals correspond with practices that are contrary to the teachings of the Bible,* as we will see more fully in chapter 14. Those who follow Jesus must closely evaluate what practices they can be involved in without compromising their faith.

During our research, we studied Wiccan books, read about Wicca and related organizations online, and talked with people involved in the craft. Each time we picked up a book or contacted someone involved in Wicca, we would pray and ask for wisdom to stay true to our faith.

For example, at one point, I (Dillon) almost created my own account at Witchvox.com to better correspond with practicing Wiccans. Yet when I read the disclaimer page, some of the expectations were clearly outside of my beliefs and biblical mandates that I cherish. Rather than compromise on what many may consider a small detail, I e-mailed Witchvox's publicity staff person and contacted individuals as a guest without becoming a member.

Of course, this process goes far beyond online affiliations. As a result of my faith, I would not be okay with someone reading my palm or doing a tarot card reading for me. However, I have built relationships with those involved in Wicca and sought to befriend them, whether or not they ever become followers of Christ.

One of my favorite stories of how God can work in the lives of those involved in Wicca is in Dan Kimball's book *They Like Jesus, but Not the Church:*

> I once sat in on a class in our church about various world faiths. When we got to the part about witchcraft and pagan religion, a twenty-four-year-old girl raised her hand. She shared that she had a Wiccan background and had become a Christian just a few months earlier. She encouraged the teachers of the class, saying that what they are teaching is important for people to understand. Of course, I was thrilled with what she said, so I talked with her afterward. It turned out that she had been heavily into witchcraft and magick. She had even joined a coven and had worked at a local witchcraft store. She had been downtown around

Easter when our church had an outdoor art event during which we had displayed the stations of the cross on the sidewalk and had pamphlets about our church available for people to pick up. She ended up visiting our website and read about our vision and who we are. She eventually started coming to our Sunday night worship gatherings right from her job at the witchcraft store. I find that so fascinating, getting off work at the witchcraft store, and then going to a church worship gathering! Through time, she ended up putting her faith in Jesus and was baptized during our evening service.[19]

God created each of us to desire a relationship with Him. To paraphrase the French philosopher Blaise Pascal, each person is hard-wired with a God-shaped vacuum in his or her heart. This vacuum makes us long for a powerful, personal relationship with the living God of the Bible. Wiccans are still searching for that relationship.

The story we just shared demonstrates how God can use all people, including Wiccans, to bring about His divine purposes in the world. True, Wiccans possess beliefs and participate in rituals that are outside of Christian boundaries. But by showing genuine love and concern for them, we have the opportunity to demonstrate the depth of God's grace and to help them fill the dark void in their lives with the light of Jesus Christ.

In Gods and Goddesses We Trust

Wicca and the Divine

"Wicca...recognizes Deity as dual. It reveres both the Goddess and the God. They are equal, warm and loving, not distant or resident in 'heaven' but omnipresent throughout the universe."

—Scott Cunningham[1]

W hen asked how she chose to follow Wicca, Jennifer shared this compelling story:

> In ninth grade, my best friend was having a crisis of faith. She'd never believed anything before, she didn't understand how our friends could be Christian, and she was on her own search for God, when we came across *Teen Witch* by Silver RavenWolf...which was, of course, all about Wicca. She showed it to me, and I thought I'd humor her (Witch-craft, how silly, right?)...so I helped her to buy it since she didn't have enough money.
>
> She read it, and a week later went around calling herself a Witch. Then over breakfast at McDonald's, she started telling me all about this religion where there's a Goddess and women are encouraged to be leaders and empowered and there's a deep connection to nature and magic...and it struck a chord deep within me. It was everything I'd always believed, but never had the words for, or a structure. So I took the book from her, and it went from there.
>
> I read another book, and one morning I was *really!* upset

and I prayed to the Goddess for the first time…and it was the first time I'd ever truly felt anything divine. It was like being wrapped in my mother's arms, but…more. I knew then that I was to be Her daughter and priestess. And that's how I got involved. I read a few more books, spent time in nature, went on Witchvox.com and found mentors and a teacher who later initiated me, and now I teach.[2]

Jennifer's story reveals several crucial elements of the Wiccan belief system, including the elevation and worship of the Goddess. It also highlights how strong the "personal relationship" factor can be in influencing others to choose the Wiccan faith.

Yes, Wiccans believe in a God, but not the God of Christianity, Judaism, or Islam. By one definition, a pagan is a person who does not follow one of these three major world religions.

Wiccan teachings propose a Goddess and a God that exist together, possess equal power, have both a "light" (good) and a "dark" (evil) side, and express themselves in a variety of ways through nature. Wiccans also call the God and the Goddess "the One," "the Lord and Lady," or "the All." Wiccans believe that the Deity is immanent (able to be experienced or known) and transcendent. They also believe that every living entity has a spirit that is connected to and part of every other spirit, and that humans are a part of nature. In addition, Wiccans believe that divinity manifests itself through all living beings and that the God and Goddess exist as aspects of a greater divinity.[3]

Wicca centers on the protection and worship of the God, the Goddess, and nature. Because most of nature is divided into male and female genders, the deities also are male and female. Wiccans' worship of these "twin" or "complementary" deities reflects the dichotomies and cycles of nature: day and night, summer and winter, planting and harvest, birth and death, and so on.

The Goddess

Many Wiccans, especially women, focus their worship almost exclusively on the Goddess. However, Jessica (not her real name) informed me (Marla) that the Wiccan worship system is similar to that of Catholicism: Catholics pray to the saints, asking them to convey those prayers to God the Father and to Mary, the mother of Jesus. Similarly, Wiccan worshipers direct their prayers to the lower gods and goddesses of the pantheon (including the deities of Greek, Roman, Celtic, and Egyptian mythology), and they ask these gods and goddesses to carry their prayers to the Goddess and the God.

"I mostly stick with the Egyptian, Celtic, and Greek pantheons," Jessica said. "Most of their deities are goddesses. For some reason, I've always been fascinated with ancient Egypt. I taught myself to write in hieroglyphics when I was four years old. And I have a lot of Scottish and Irish blood in my family."

RESPONSES *to* PRAYER

Jessica told me that she directs her prayers primarily to three goddesses: Hecate, Aphrodite, and Bastet. She believes these goddesses will then convey her prayers to the Goddess and the God. "But the Goddess and the God may or may not answer," she said matter-of-factly.

The Wiccan Goddess, sometimes called Gaia or Diana, is described as the universal mother:

> She is the source of fertility, endless wisdom and loving caresses. As the Wicca know Her, She is often of three aspects: the Maiden, the Mother and the Crone, symbolized in the waxing, full and waning of the Moon. She is at once the unploughed field, the full harvest and the dormant, frost-covered Earth. She gives birth to abundance... Since the Goddess is nature, all nature, She is both the Temptress and the Crone; the tornado and the fresh spring rain; the cradle and the grave...No matter how we envision Her, She is omnipresent, changeless, eternal.[4]

Wiccans revere the Goddess as the giver of love, the provider of abundance, and the creator of fertility. She reigns over the moon, the sea, and the earth. In Wiccan literature, the Goddess may be depicted as "a huntress running with Her hounds; a celestial deity striding across the sky with stardust falling from Her heels; the eternal Mother heavy with child; the weaver of our lives and deaths; and a Crone walking by waning moonlight seeking out the weak and forlorn."[5]

Although Wiccans say they believe that the God is equal to the Goddess, I (Marla) noticed that the God was rarely mentioned in my conversations with Wiccans. Most Wiccans, especially women, relate more closely with the concept of a female Goddess than with that of a male God. However:

> The Goddess and God are equal; neither is higher or more deserving of respect. Though some Wiccans focus their rituals toward the Goddess and seem to forget the God entirely, this is a reaction to centuries of stifling patriarchal religion, and the loss of acknowledgement of the feminine aspect of Divinity. Religion based entirely on feminine energy, however, is as unbalanced and unnatural as one totally masculine in focus. The ideal is a perfect balance of the two. The Goddess and God are equal, complementary.[6]

Edain McCoy expresses his belief this way: "We worship a deity that is both male and female, a mother Goddess and father God, who together created all that is, was, or will be. We respect life, cherish the free will of sentient beings, and accept the sacredness of all creation."[7]

As a woman, I understand the powerful allure of the Goddess, especially for young women coming of age in our postmodern culture. The idea of casting off thousands of years of limiting traditions and patriarchal practices within the church is appealing. But Wiccans' ideas and writings about the Goddess reflect several misconceptions about the Bible and Christianity.

Probably the greatest misconception is that God is male. The Bible does use male pronouns to refer to God, but He is a Spirit, not a human. He is *not* a man, nor is He a woman. Noted Hebrew scholar Kenneth Boa writes,

> In actual fact the Bible does not teach that God is male, but rather views God as an incorporeal spirit who transcends all created distinctions and who is neither male nor female. As if to underscore this point, the Old Testament explicitly denies that God is either male or human: "God is not a man [Hebrew *ish*, a male adult], that He should lie, nor a son of man [*ish*], that He should repent" (Num. 23:19). Nor is God human at all: "For He is not a man [Hebrew *'adam*, human being], that he should relent" (1 Sam. 15:29). The Bible clearly reveals God to be an infinite Spirit whom the universe itself cannot contain (1 Kings 8:27; John 4:24; Acts 7:49; 17:24).[8]

Interestingly, the Bible contains many verses that also attribute characteristics to God and to Jesus that we might consider traditionally female. Both the Father and Son are portrayed as nurturing, relational, loving, compassionate, slow to anger, and forgiving. When Jesus looked out over the city of Jerusalem, His heart broke over the people's hardness of heart. He wept over the city, saying, "O Jerusalem, Jerusalem, you who kill the prophets and stone those sent to you, how often I have longed to gather your children together, as a hen gathers her chicks under her wings, but you were not willing" (Matthew 23:37; Luke 13:34).

In some ways, the loving care, mercy, and protection that the Father and Son offer could be considered womanly or motherly characteristics. God created men and women in His image, so it makes sense that He would demonstrate some of the characteristics that are also displayed by both men and women, though God Himself is neither male nor female. Clearly, He values both male and female attributes very highly—and so should we!

Below, we'll discuss several more aspects of the God and the Goddess and explore some additional differences between the Wiccan deities and the God of the Bible.

The God

Who is the God of Wicca? He is often called Gaius, the Green Man, the Horned God, or Pan. One Wiccan states, "The God has been revered for eons. He is neither the stern, all-powerful deity of Christianity and Judaism, nor is He simply the consort of the Goddess. God or Goddess, they are equal, one."[9]

The God of Wicca is represented by the sun and the fully ripened harvest. His vast domain includes the deserts, the forests, the mountains, and even the stars. He also tends the wild animals. He is the God of procreation, and sexuality is openly celebrated in Wicca as a pleasurable aspect of nature. The God is known as the Sky Father, who is thought to have descended upon the Earth Mother (the Goddess) and united with her to form the All.

Wiccans believe that both the God and the Goddess possess a dark side, in contrast with the God of the Bible. Scripture says, "God is light; in him there is no darkness at all" (1 John 1:5). Scott Cunningham writes,

> We acknowledge the dark aspects of the Goddess and the God as well as the bright. All nature is composed of opposites, and this polarity is also resident within ourselves. The darkest human traits as well as the brightest are locked within our unconsciousness. It is only our ability to rise above destructive urges, to channel such energies into positive thoughts and actions, that separates us from mass-murderers and sociopaths.[10]

This view reflects an attitude similar to that expressed in Greek and Roman mythology. The Greek and Roman gods acted in ways contrary to God Almighty as revealed in the Bible. Greek and Roman gods were superhuman but flawed, powerful but capricious, giving but also self-centered, loving but murderous and insanely jealous at times. They used people and the other gods to fulfill their own desires as they acted out a larger-than-life play on the stage of heaven and earth. They acted like glorified humans, simply living their lives on a cosmic scale. Not surprising, since they were invented by humans!

How Is the Concept of the Goddess Flawed?

Pagan goddess worship has occurred for millennia. The Bible mentions several ancient goddesses by name, including Ashtoreth and Artemis (see 1 Kings 11:5,33; 2 Kings 23:13; and Acts 19:27,37). However, the writers of Scripture adamantly warned God's people to refrain completely from the worship of goddesses and idols. Those who did not, including King Solomon, faced severe and painful consequences.

Solomon first got himself into trouble by marrying the daughter of the pharaoh of Egypt. The Egyptians worshiped a pantheon of gods and goddesses, and Solomon's wife led his heart away from the Lord, prompting him to offer sacrifices to her false idols. He also began to take other pagan wives. According to 1 Kings 11, "King Solomon…loved many foreign women besides Pharaoh's daughter… They were from nations about which the LORD had told the Israelites, 'You must not intermarry with them, because they will surely turn your hearts after their gods.' Nevertheless, Solomon held fast to them in love" (verses 1-2). God grew angry with Solomon and chose to remove the rulership of the kingdom of Israel from Solomon's son because Solomon's heart had turned away from Him (see 1 Kings 11:11-12).

Another issue involves the power of the Goddess and the God to act in people's lives. Cunningham again states,

> The Goddess and God…can be called upon to help us
> sort through the vicissitudes of our existences and bring
> joy into our often spiritually-bereft lives. [But] this doesn't

mean that when problems occur we should leave them in the hands of the Goddess. This is a stalling maneuver, an avoidance of dealing with the bumps on the road of life. However, as Wiccans we can call on the Goddess and God to clear our minds and to *help us help ourselves*. Magic is an excellent means of accomplishing this. After attuning with the Goddess and God, Wiccans ask Their assistance during the magical rite that usually follows.[11]

In contrast, the Bible teaches us that we *can* leave our problems in God's hands. The Bible urges us to "cast all your anxiety on [God] because he cares for you" (1 Peter 5:7) and to

> cast your cares on the LORD
> and he will sustain you;
> he will never let the righteous fall (Psalm 55:22).

If a person can't trust the Goddess to work in his or her life, then she must not have any real power (or at least she must not be very dependable)! If the way to solve your problem is to clear your mind and *help yourself*, then the Goddess hasn't done anything for you at all. In that case, all you needed was the motivation to solve your own problem.

Truth is, if we could help ourselves out of every tough situation, we wouldn't need God in the first place. But He created us to be in relationship with Him, dependent on Him for even our daily bread. Dependent on Him for salvation, for blessing, for life.

Wiccan tradition teaches that the Goddess and the God are equal, yet it also teaches that the Goddess "created" or "gave birth" to the God. It would seem that the God would therefore possess less power and authority than the Goddess.

But, some Wiccans might say, doesn't the Bible assert that a human mother named Mary give birth to Jesus? And wasn't He God? Yes, Jesus was the Messiah, the second Person of the Trinity, fully God and fully man. He loved people with incredible compassion; He taught with great wisdom; He offered people the gift of salvation; and He performed miraculous signs to demonstrate that He truly was the Son of God.

The Bible emphasizes that Jesus was *not created* by God the Father. He existed in eternity past with the other persons of the Triune God. "In the beginning was the Word [Jesus], and the Word was with God, and the Word was God. He was with God in the beginning. Through him all things were made...In him was life, and that life was the light of men" (John 1:1-4).

How Is the Concept of the God Flawed?

The Wiccan concept of the God and Goddess differs significantly from that of the God of the Bible. The following chart offers just a sampling of what we know about God the Father, both from *special revelation* (the Scriptures) and from *natural revelation* (what we know and understand about God from nature).

The God of the Bible Is...

The Creator of heaven and earth (including animals and people)	Genesis 1:1–2:25; Isaiah 40:28
Eternal	Genesis 1:1-2; 21:33; Deuteronomy 33:27
Omnipresent (present everywhere at once; always with us)	Psalm 139:6-10
Greater than all other gods	Exodus 18:11; 2 Chronicles 2:5
Omnipotent (all-powerful)	Exodus 32:11; Job 30:18; Psalm 66:3; Jeremiah 32:18
Compassionate and gracious, slow to anger, abounding in love and faithfulness	Exodus 34:6; Numbers 14:18
Not a man; does not lie or change His mind	Numbers 23:19; Job 33:12

A consuming fire, a jealous God	Deuteronomy 4:24; Hebrews 12:29
Merciful and forgiving	Deuteronomy 4:31; Daniel 9:9
One—and there is no other but Him; the only true God	Deuteronomy 6:4; Jeremiah 10:10; Mark 12:32; John 17:3; Galatians 3:20
Faithful, keeping His covenant of love to a thousand generations of those who love Him and keep His commands	Deuteronomy 7:9; 2 Corinthians 1:18
Testing us to find out whether we love Him with all our heart and soul	Deuteronomy 13:3
Our stronghold, refuge, and savior	2 Samuel 22:2; Psalm 18:2
Gracious and compassionate; will not turn His face from us if we return to Him	2 Chronicles 30:9
Omniscient (all-knowing); full of wisdom	1 Samuel 2:3; Job 12:13; 1 John 3:20
Mighty and firm in His purpose	Job 36:5
A righteous judge; present in the company of the righteous	Psalm 7:11; 14:5
Our shepherd	Psalm 23:1
Holy; seated on His holy throne	Psalm 47:8; 99:9
The only source of our salvation; our salvation comes from Him	Psalm 62:1; Isaiah 12:2
The potter; we are all the work of His hand	Isaiah 64:8
The God of gods and the Lord of kings and a revealer of mysteries	Daniel 2:47
Spirit; and His worshipers must worship in spirit and in truth	John 4:24
The only true God	Jeremiah 10:10; John 17:3

Invisible, though His eternal power and divine nature have been clearly seen from what has been made, so that we are without excuse	Romans 1:20
Not a God of disorder but of peace	1 Corinthians 14:33
Able to make all grace abound to us, so that we will abound in every good work	2 Corinthians 9:8
The Father of the heavenly lights, who does not change like shifting shadows	James 1:17
Patient with us, not wanting anyone to perish, but everyone to come to repentance	2 Peter 3:9
Light; in Him there is no darkness at all	1 John 1:5
Love—whoever lives in love lives in God, and God in him	1 John 4:8,16
The Alpha and the Omega, who is, and who was, and who is to come, the Almighty	Revelation 1:8
Worthy to receive glory and honor and power, for He created all things, and by His will they were created and have their being	Revelation 4:11

These Scripture verses reveal that God is Almighty, existing in eternity and outside of time. His power, majesty, and righteousness are unparalleled. Man can establish a relationship with God, but man cannot fathom all of God's ways. God exists as the Trinity (Father, Son, and Holy Spirit), separate from humans, yet loving them and desiring a personal relationship with each person He has created.

According to Wicca, however, the Goddess and the God have "been in us and around us all the time; we need only open ourselves to this awareness. This is one of the secrets of Wicca—Deity dwells within."[12] This view reflects a pantheistic perspective, suggesting that God exists in everything.

The Wiccan concept of the equal Goddess and the God, both possessing a dark side that balances their light side, suggests another theological fallacy: that of the *duality* of good and evil in the world. An easy way to understand this concept is by picturing the ongoing battle between good and evil in the movie *Star Wars*. Luke Skywalker is good, but not perfect; Darth Vader is evil, but possesses some good qualities. Both possess great power and use "the Force" to attempt to achieve their purposes. The concept of duality suggests that *the forces of good and evil possess equal power; one will never win out over the other.* The battle will continue to rage, and no supremely powerful absolute good exists to conquer absolute evil.

This fallacy, when applied to Christian doctrine, suggests that God and Satan's power are equal and therefore cancel each other out; neither is more powerful than the other. However, the Bible clearly states that God *is* more powerful than Satan and that God will conquer Satan in the end and cast him into the lake of fire for eternity. Satan does have a measure of power, though, as the "prince of this world." He seeks to lead people away from the truth as a method of getting back at God and thwarting God's purposes. But God will eventually step in and end Satan's reign of power on earth.

Starhawk refers to some of the concepts mentioned above when she writes,

> Each individual is a living embodiment of the sacred. The divine experience is equally available to all, and each person's experience of the divine is valid and important. Spiritual authority is located within us. We are each keepers of our own conscience...
>
> Because we value freedom of thought, we accept no dogmas nor implement any required beliefs. We do, however, have a working model of the universe that includes interconnected realms of matter and spirit. Most of us prefer the term "Goddess" for the weaver of this web, but we also recognize

an eclectic pantheon of Goddesses and Gods, each of them particular constellations of power, with whom we are co-creators of change and fate. At the heart of the cosmos is mystery, that which can never be defined nor controlled.[13]

Mystery doesn't belong to Wicca alone. It's a crucial element of the Christian faith as well. *The Message* paraphrases the words of the apostle Paul: "This Christian life is a great mystery, far exceeding our understanding, but some things are clear enough: [Jesus Christ] appeared in a human body, was proved right by the invisible Spirit, was seen by angels. He was proclaimed among all kinds of peoples, believed in all over the world, taken up into heavenly glory" (1 Timothy 3:16 MSG).

Paul also wrote to the believers at Ephesus, "The mystery is that people who have never heard of God and those who have heard of him all their lives (what I've been calling outsiders and insiders) stand on the same ground before God. They get the same offer, same help, same promises in Christ Jesus. The Message is accessible and welcoming to everyone, across the board" (Ephesians 3:6 MSG).

The gospel message overflows with mystery, wonder, and grace. Sadly, many of us have lost our sense of awe and mystery when it comes to our relationship with God. We're afraid to admit that there are attributes of God that we cannot fathom or explain on this side of eternity. If we were to admit that, we'd go a long way in being able to relate better to Wiccans!

The God Who Answers Prayer

As I mentioned earlier, Jessica told me, "The Goddess and the God may or may not answer your prayers." But the true God, our heavenly Father, *always* answers our prayers. And when He does, He gives one of three answers:

1. *Yes!* I'll do it.

2. *No!* There's a reason why this is not best for you. You may

not see or understand the reason now, but you will discover it in time. Trust Me.

3. *Wait!* Now is not the right time. Be patient, keep praying, and wait to see what I am going to do in your life.

The Scriptures emphasize the importance of prayer—and they also assert God's awesome power to answer. God said,

> He will call upon me, and I will answer him;
> I will be with him in trouble,
> I will deliver him and honor him (Psalm 91:15).

Another verse assures us, "The earnest prayer of a righteous person has great power and produces wonderful results" (James 5:16 NLT).

Through prayer, we see God work in extraordinary ways in our lives. Through prayer, we're reminded of our sinfulness and frailty. Through prayer, we have the privilege of pouring out the depths of our souls to the One who has the power to redeem our sin and change our lives. And He will be faithful to answer when we call on Him!

In this chapter, we've addressed Wicca's approach to the divine. In chapter 7, we'll discuss some of the women involved in Wicca and determine why Wicca appeals to so many women in today's postmodern culture.

The Feminine Factor

The Women of Wicca

"We find in the Goddess a compelling image of female power, a vision of the deep connection of all beings in the web of life, and a call to create peace on earth."

—CAROL CHRIST[1]

I(Marla) met Vanessa (not her real name) in my creative writing class on the first day of my last semester at Purdue University. I strolled into class, plopped my heavy book bag down on the table, and introduced myself. "Hi, I'm Marla."

"I'm Vanessa, and I'm a white witch," she said.

I stared at her in surprise. I'd never met a witch before—not that I was aware of, anyway—but this tall, pretty girl with long, straight auburn hair didn't match my idea of what a witch should look like.

Throughout the semester, as we progressed in our writing and shared it with the group, I began to recognize some unresolved anger and hurts in Vanessa's life. I realized that these emotions might have motivated her to seek out Wicca as a means of making her feel powerful, confident, and in control of her destiny. She often seemed defiant, and she and her friend Kyle, who had also enrolled in the class, seemed to enjoy poking fun at other people and their writing.

Several members of the class were Christians, and although we did not write preachy or explicitly Christian work, we did sometimes use biblical themes and spiritual concepts in our writing. Vanessa was disdainful of this. Because I wasn't sure how to engage with someone claiming to be a witch, I didn't spend much time interacting with her or trying to understand her point of view on spiritual matters.

I attended church at the Christian Campus House on Purdue's campus. On my last Sunday there, just before graduation, our college pastor announced that he had gone around campus and recorded random, unscripted video interviews with students. He asked each of them just one question: "What do you believe in?"

The pastor rolled the video. Tears began to stream down my cheeks as I heard one student after another offer answers that had nothing to do with God:

"I believe I have the power to change the world."

"I believe in hard work and determination."

"I believe in the American dream."

"I believe education is the answer to our nation's problems."

When the last video clip flashed on the screen, I gasped out loud.

"What do you believe in?" our pastor was asking Vanessa.

"I believe in myself!" she asserted, eyes flashing. "I believe I have the power to attain my goals. I can achieve whatever I want to achieve, and no one can hold me back!"

A wave of regret washed over me as I realized I should have taken the time to get to know Vanessa and share my faith with her, to tell her the reason for my hope in God. Now, it was too late.

Thankfully, God used that experience to plant a seed in my heart. Little did I know that about ten years later, I would be writing a book on Wicca to help others understand this religion and how to reach out to those like Vanessa who practice it. He gave me another chance to minister to pagans, and this time, I took it.

Why the Appeal?

Wicca and other New Age religions hold special appeal for women, partly because these religions emphasize the sacred feminine. In other religions, the role, value, and participation of women is limited; but in Wicca, women are highly valued and even worshipped as daughters of the Goddess and the God. In fact, in Wicca, the Goddess is considered to be equal to the God, if not even more approachable and powerful, because she created him (according to Wicca's creation story).

Many of today's world religions do not allow women to hold high leadership positions; but in Wicca, women may serve as high priestesses and coven leaders, and they enjoy great prestige and status as spiritual mentors and guides.

How many women are involved in Wicca? Obtaining an accurate count is difficult because many pagans choose not to list Wicca as their religious preference on surveys. In her article "Weak Church, Wiccan Charms," Catherine Edwards Sanders writes,

> Statistics tell us that two-thirds of practicing Pagans are women. Estimates of the total numbers of practicing Wiccans in America vary wildly, as people can be reluctant to reveal their spiritual inclination publicly. Conservative estimates put the number at somewhere between 150,000 and 200,000. A poll conducted by a large Pagan group put the number at almost 800,000, while some Wiccans claim there are as many as 3 million of them. These numbers reveal a growing spiritual hunger for something that is not being met by traditional means.[2]

One Wiccan wrote,

> You can't really put a figure on women vs. men in the community because we are still by and large quite secretive due to misunderstandings and religious persecution. I do think it's safe to say that the number of women is larger than the number of men, perhaps significantly so, and it is also safe to say that there is a disproportionately large population of homosexuals who practice Wicca since we do not consider it to be evil to be gay...Also, I would say it is safe to say there are more women than men because Wicca is a religion that holds women as equals to men, spiritual leaders,

and we have a distinct and revered feminine divine that is not subservient to another divine source.[3]

As we move further into the twenty-first century, the number of women involved in Wicca continues to skyrocket. You may not realize it, but most likely, you encounter pagans and witches everywhere you go: at school, at stores and restaurants, at work, at social functions and meetings, at your university, at community events. The military women you see on leave may be Wiccan, because the armed forces officially recognize Wicca as a religion (as an example, see the sidebar below). You may even be encountering witches at church! Over the next few years, you may have several opportunities to engage these people in meaningful conversations about God, values, life, and faith.

IN *the* MILITARY

Because of Wicca's official status in the armed forces, we find material like this in the U.S. Army's *Handbook for Chaplains:* "Wiccans employ such means as dance, chant, creative visualization and hypnosis to focus and direct psychic energy for the purpose of healing, protecting and aiding members in various endeavors."[4]

The Desire for Acceptance

Sadly, many women involved in Wicca have faced hurtful attacks, persecution, and misunderstanding from Christians rather than feeling that those Christ followers love them and care about them. Consider this story from a Wiccan named Maplecrow, who worked with a group of Christians:

> One day, I decided to have lunch with the group. A discussion about religion popped up. It was very uncomfortable. I told my co-worker that I didn't need to be a Christian and that I wasn't.
>
> That person, who I will call Mr. D., changed his demeanor

with me after that. I never ate lunch with the group if I could avoid it. Mr. D. even brought up, while in the office, how "women have never been powerful in history." That made a lot of the ladies upset; some people decided to debate him.

But no one went to Human Resources.

Over time, I began to wear my pentacle. I placed my goddess, green-man, and pagan décor on my desk. No one said anything to me until one day, during break, Mr. D. and another co-worker looked at some question puzzles.

One of the puzzle questions was about the moon. I tried to help find the answer and drew on the white board a crescent moon.

While my back was turned to the board, I heard Mr. D. distinctly say "Witch!"

I turned around to look at Mr. D. and found him stammering in a nervous manner while staring at me. (The other co-worker joining us has a distinct accent, so there was no mistake in noting who said it.)

It didn't stop there.

One lady, who worked down the hall from our offices, used her finger to cross my forehead and the back of my neck with a Christian cross. She told me she prayed for me always.

Why?

I was a deer caught in the headlights—just plain shocked by what she had done. I was only dropping by her office to say hello and give her news of my day, not to instigate any religious confrontation.

Eventually, my new boss called me in. I did my best to share my concerns with him about how I felt working in his department. He didn't even listen. He told me that I wasn't very good in my chosen educational degree field and that I should think about becoming something else.[5]

Catherine Edwards Sanders tells the story of Rebecca (not her real name), another woman who feels marginalized by society. "My place in society has become so altered. I work, I contribute, but I have become invisible," she laments to a friend. A nurse and a mother of grown children, Rebecca has just had a hysterectomy. She uses ritual in a small outdoor ceremony to deal with feelings of loss after the surgery and to seek direction. After taking off her clothes, she covers herself with red-clay rune symbols and buries the organs removed from surgery in part of her wedding dress. She and her friend perform a Wiccan ritual. They both play flutes and place crystals and a feather on the burial spot.[6]

Some of these rituals seem so foreign to those of us who are Christians. What could cause a person to embrace this lifestyle and engage in such unusual rituals and practices? Basically, the desire for *acceptance*. These women desperately searched for their place in the world and within the church, but they struggled to find it. However, when they discovered Wicca, they finally felt like they *belonged*. They embraced a cafeteria-style religion that was not regimented and patriarchal. They felt free to worship the Goddess and the God as they pleased. And, perhaps most important, they felt loved and accepted by others in their religious community.

A Wiccan high priestess I (Marla) spoke with said, "Wicca embraces the Goddess, for she is our Divine Mother to which women can relate because of the maiden, mother, and crone stages of a woman. The God is important, as well, but we embrace them both, unlike the Christians in worshiping an all-dominating male figure."[7]

Margot Adler said that in the course of writing her book on neopaganism, she met a woman who told her, "Just the idea of a [Mother] Goddess and I felt this great weight drop from me. I felt the last prejudices against my female body falling away."[8]

Another author wrote, "I met many women who had been deeply wounded by a church experience and considered Wicca to be a safe place for them."[9]

As a Christian, I'm saddened when I hear these words. I feel compelled to reach out more to women like those mentioned in this chapter. I sense God's desire to make the church a place that welcomes people of all faiths and all walks of life and provides them with the opportunity to discover His truth. Together, we can commit to making the church a safer, more positive, and more welcoming place for those whose lives need to be transformed by God's message of salvation.

Jesus, Women, and Wicca

Roberta became a Christian in her youth. After her conversion, she attended a Christian camp one summer on Catalina Island in California. There, she began to lead a Bible study in the local coffee shop in town. Throughout the summer, people in the coffee shop came to know Christ. Roberta was thrilled, but word of this Bible study soon filtered to camp leaders, and the men in charge told her that she would no longer be able to lead this study because she was a woman. A man had to take over. So a man did, and the Bible study soon fizzled.

Roberta had several other experiences like this within evangelical circles. She was discouraged, but other Christian men and women encouraged her to stick with it. She knew from the Bible that Jesus had elevated women despite the custom of the time. So Roberta persevered and is a faithful Christian today.

Roberta joined World Vision, a Christian relief organization, and in 1987, she became president of a Christian college. Roberta is an example of someone who became a Christian as feminism was on the rise. She faced disappointment and discouragement in her Christian walk, but she managed to persevere in her faith and become a powerful example to men and women all over the world. How? She looked to the person and work of Jesus Christ for truth and solace when she felt hurt by the words and actions of Christians around her.[10]

Many women, however, struggle to cling to their Christian faith in the face of such painful experiences. Sometimes, these women turn to Wicca and witchcraft when they are hurt by Christians or others who may or may not have been part of the church.

Why do Christians alienate these seekers? The Bible teaches us to do just the opposite. The clear evidence of our God, our faith, and our lives should make the gospel irresistible to those all around us.

In addition, the Bible is not as patriarchal as some people would like us to believe. Jesus reflected the heart of God by treating women with great honor and respect. His interactions with women were so surprising and compelling that they caused a great deal of consternation among His disciples as well as among the religious leaders of His day. When Jesus met the woman at the well, He praised her and taught her rather than condemning her. He allowed another "sinful" woman to pour an expensive ointment on His feet in the company of others. He loved and honored His mother, Mary. He became fast friends with Mary and Martha of Bethany and loved them deeply— He even raised their brother, Lazarus, from the dead!

The apostle Paul also interacted often with women involved in the early church. In Romans 16:1, he wrote, "I commend to you our sister Phoebe, a servant of the church in Cenchrea." He began the personal greetings portion of this vital New Testament letter with a statement of recommendation and high recognition for Phoebe, a godly and influential woman in the early church. The New Testament also mentions a variety of other women who played active roles in the Christian church, including Priscilla, Lois, Eunice, Dorcas, Lydia, Susanna, Joanna, Mary the mother of Jesus, Mary and Martha of Bethany, and Mary Magdalene. Several of these were wealthy women of great status in their communities who provided financial support, food, lodging, and protection to Jesus, the apostles, and other early church leaders.

The Bible encourages us to love each other and to treat our brothers and sisters with high regard. According to 1 John,

> If someone says, "I love God," but hates a Christian brother
> or sister, that person is a liar; for if we don't love people

> we can see, how can we love God, whom we cannot see?
> And he has given us this command: Those who love God
> must also love their Christian brothers and sisters (1 John
> 4:20-21 NLT).

We're called to love God as well as each other—and not just those people who are Christians, but everyone.

Scripture reminds us that "God's kindness leads you toward repentance" (Romans 2:4). More than anything else, Jesus' love and kindness drew people irresistibly to Him. Throngs of people flocked around Him everywhere He went. A woman who had suffered from an ailment for many years reached out to touch the hem of His robe, trusting that just touching Jesus' clothing for an instant would enable her to be healed. And it did!

In the same way, it's our kindness and care for those of other faiths that will draw them to the Lord. If we are harsh and judgmental, we will only drive people away. You may have only one chance—one touch—to help transform a life. Speak words of life rather than words of condemnation.

All around us, women like Vanessa, Starhawk, Maplecrow, Rebecca, and Roberta are searching for significance in their lives—women desperately in need of forgiveness, love, acceptance, mercy, and grace. Women longing to discover the truth—yet being led deeper and deeper into falsehood. It's up to us to do something about it.

In the next chapter, you'll read the remarkable story of a young woman who became involved with Wicca, went Goth, quit school, moved to Hollywood (where she lived in abject poverty in a roach-infested hotel room), and got pulled into a shocking downward spiral that almost destroyed her life.

Until God stepped in.

"I Was a Witch"

The Story of Former Craft Practitioner Kimberly Shumate

*"For pity's sake, don't 'tell' [your children] what religion is and is not.
Let them discover spirituality for themselves...
WitchCraft isn't something that you need to worry about.
Celebrate that your child seeks empowerment."*

—Silver RavenWolf, from
"Introduction: Just for Parents" in *Teen Witch*

During our discussions with current and former adherents of the craft, I (Dillon) discovered that an acquaintance of mine had been heavily involved in witchcraft and Wicca. After talking with her about her experiences, I obtained permission to share an earlier article she penned on the subject. We have included it here in its entirety to help provide insight into the life of a person who was deeply involved in Wicca but later chose to place her faith in Jesus Christ.

We hope Kimberly's amazing story will inspire you and provide you with tools you can use in your discussions with those involved in the craft or other New Age religions.

Witchcraft, telepathy, levitation, spirit channeling, ESP, and a host of other paranormal activities were all I knew from early childhood. While we attended church every Sunday and called ourselves

Christians, my parents started espousing Hindu beliefs and New Age philosophies. Soon, choir camp was replaced with psychic camp, and séances, Ouija boards, crystals, and pendulums became the norm in our home. Every night around the dinner table, we discussed topics such as ghosts, poltergeists, and contact from the beyond. Yet as strange as it sounds, we still considered ourselves to be Christian.

Then, when I was 17, my mother's slow, agonizing battle with cancer ended. The void within me was too great to fill, so I found solace in my anger. To anesthetize my pain over my mom's death, I turned to black magic, voodoo, hexes, and curses. Since my future seemed so uncertain, I began reading tarot cards to tell my fortune. I even took on a new appearance—I cut and dyed my light brown curls jet black. I wore white makeup, black lipstick, and black clothes. Eight holes pierced my ear—my new trademark.

My behavior changed as well. I quit high school and started hanging out downtown with all the other misfits and vagabonds. One of my best friends was a warlock named Stephen. Witchcraft became my haven, my identity, my lifestyle. Although my dad and I were close, he was too caught up in his grief to seem to notice the poor choices I was making. He later told me he was sorry he hadn't been more of an emotional support for me during the time my life started taking its downward spiral.

THE ROAD MANY PEOPLE TAKE

It is possible to become a student in a Wiccan church right now at Wicca.org.

I considered myself a spiritual person. While I believed God is the Creator of all things and that Jesus Christ is His Son, one important element was missing: reverence. I had no fear of God, no sense of accountability or responsibility to Him. In my mind, hell didn't exist, which alleviated the consequences of evil.

As the years went by, I barely scraped out a living as a manicurist.

I moved from place to place—Atlanta, Seattle, and finally Hollywood when I was 26 years old. With no money, no car, and no telephone, life was hard. The tiny room I rented on the Boulevard was hot and cockroach-infested. I stepped over used syringes and condoms each morning on my way to the bus stop. I didn't fill my father in on all these details because I didn't want him to worry. I persisted in romanticizing this colorful and sometimes dangerous lifestyle, but it was taking its toll.

Suffering from severe anorexia, my 100-pound, 5-foot-5-inch frame had its share of health issues. And with a weekly budget of fifty dollars, as the years passed, I wondered why the Universe wasn't taking better care of me. Surely the answer lay within the supernatural sphere of my mother's crystal ball, which my father gave me right after she died. Though it was quite large and expensive, the thought of selling it never crossed my mind, as it would inevitably become a family heirloom. Still, whenever I gazed into it, I received no word from the beyond. I sank deeper into poverty, and my health problems progressed.

A stark contrast to my growing misery was Joyce, a woman who frequented the salon where I worked. Her deep, sincere joy baffled me. I was in turmoil emotionally and physically, and unfulfilled spiritually. I wondered what Joyce had found that I'd overlooked. She didn't shove her Christian beliefs down my throat, but planted a seed by saying, "You need to come to my church."

I remember the first time I took her up on that offer. The service was held in the auditorium of a junior high school. I'd never seen people like those in attendance that morning—hands raised, singing, smiling. It was too much for me to take, so I left and didn't return for several months.

In the interim, I tried everything I'd missed the prior 29 years of searching, until there was nothing left to try. The Buddhists and the Hindus didn't offer the joy and peace I glimpsed in the people at Joyce's church. I didn't find the answers I sought in the psychic who "conversed" with angels, in the book *A Course in Miracles*, or with the Christian Scientists. The only thing I hadn't given a real try was found in that little church in the junior high. So, somewhat self-consciously and most unenthusiastically, I went back to find out more.

As I sat down, I silently shot up a desperate prayer: *God, please give me someone in this crazy crowd I can relate to. If You don't give me someone, I'm walking out of here.* At that moment, the pastor told the congregation to stand up and shake a few hands. I introduced myself to Lisa, whose dyed-red hair and nose ring suggested we might be at a similar place. My black-and-white hair and spiked belt told her the same. Lisa, a fellow spiritual seeker, and I became fast friends.

Looking back, I wonder how the church members stood having me in their midst for so long. I was angry and exasperated as I sat listening to their "good news." How could there be only *one* way to God? At the end of each message, I marched down the aisle to the pastor and began firing off an onslaught of questions. After three or four weeks of verbal sparring, he humbly offered the associate pastor's ear. I made my rounds from one elder to another, finally ending up at a Friday night Bible study looking for answers.

As I sat on the floor in the leader's living room, I felt a peace amidst this group of people who seemed to care about each other. After the study, Lisa sat beside me as Scott, the leader, patiently listened to my New-Age arguments. But one by one, the Scriptures I'd carefully prepared to punch holes in the gospel came back at me with hurricane force. Scott's words—but especially the Bible's words—confounded my cosmic view. After we'd sat there for an hour debating, I was exhausted. My hardened heart and argumentative nature finally had enough.

As Lisa drove me home, my mind ached as I replayed Scott's words. All the Old Testament and New Testament verses had one oddly familiar voice—one tone, one heart. I wondered, *How could a book written by so many different people over the course of hundreds of years fit together perfectly as if one amazing storyteller had written the whole thing?* The Holy Spirit began melting my vanity and arrogance with a power stronger than any hex, incantation, or spell I'd ever used. Suddenly, the blindfold I'd worn for almost 30 years was stripped away, and instantly I knew what I'd been searching for: *Jesus!* The same God I'd neglected, whose name I'd used as profanity, whom I'd flat-out rejected, was the one who'd sent His Son to suffer for me, to take the guilty verdict so I could be found innocent. My eyes filled with tears as I exchanged the darkness with which I'd grown so accustomed for the light of God's truth. It was such a personal moment between the Lord and me that even Lisa, sitting next to me in the car, had no idea what was going on.

I soon realized my life was filled with empty props, and it was time to clean house. My first act of obedience was to throw out all my books on witchcraft and the paranormal, as well as my tarot cards. But the most important possession—and most difficult to discard— was my treasured crystal ball.

I called Lisa. She came right over, and we immediately drove to the Pacific Ocean. My heart pounded as if the demons themselves weren't far behind us. We stood at the end of Malibu Pier, our beaming faces reflecting the radiance of the setting sun. I unwrapped the crystal's black velvet cover, and light streamed out like rainbows as the thick crystal met the sun's fleeting rays. As I dropped the ball into the deep blue water, I knew my future was secure. Now I had a Savior who would be with me always. It still moves me to tears to think He waited through all those years of anger, disappointment, fear, and bad choices. All the mistakes I'd ever made were wiped clean. It was amazing!

I'd attended church one week to argue with the members, then returned the following week in tears to pray the sinner's prayer in front of the entire congregation. It sounds astounding, but that's exactly what I did. One by one the Holy Spirit freed me from the trappings of my former life: the practice of counterfeit religions, smoking, cursing, promiscuity, drug use, lying, and believing I was worthless. My old friends filtered out, and God replaced them with incredible new ones. He took me from that one-room hovel on Hollywood Boulevard back to my hometown and the security of friends, family, and a Spirit-filled church.

By this time, my father had recommitted his life to Christ. He was thrilled I'd found Christ too, and knew it was true by the extreme change in me. A few days before he passed away from heart failure in 1997, I asked him if he would save me a place next to him at God's banquet table. He replied, "Sweetie, I wouldn't have it any other way."

My life has changed dramatically since my conversion 12 years ago. I've been healed of anorexia for several years, and I now help others with the same affliction. I hope God will open the door for me to work with others trapped by the occult as well.

There are times when I think back to my old life—the selfishness and the isolation of life without God. It reminds me of what the Enemy put me through. I wouldn't trade my new life for anything in this world.[1]

Compassion for Creation

Wicca and the Environment

I told my friend, "Only children get excited over watching a
butterfly." But then he turned to me and said, "So does God."

—STEVEN JAMES[1]

In all of my (Marla's) interactions with Wiccans, one facet of Wicca shone radiantly: Its adherents truly love nature and respect creation. They feel a deep, primal sense of communion, empathy, and oneness with the earth. I grew to have an immense respect for them, in part because of their concern for honoring and preserving this exquisite and fragile planet.

Two Alternative Religious Philosophies

Wiccans and pagans all over the world stand united in their initiative to protect the earth. Many do so because they subscribe to one of the following religious philosophies.

"It's All God"

Raymond Buckland, one of the most popular Wiccan authors, writes, "[Wicca] is a religion and a practice of nature, showing and demonstrating that we are all one and all equal—humans, animals, plants, trees; everything animate and inanimate is closely related."[2]

In contrast, the Bible teaches that God, people, animals, and nature are *not* "all one and equal." God, in the form of the Trinity, is almighty and eternal; He exists in eternity past, present, and future (see Genesis 21:33; Deuteronomy 33:27; Jeremiah 10:10; Romans 1:20). Scripture teaches us that our Father is omnipotent (all-powerful), omniscient (all-knowing), and omnipresent (present everywhere). Yet He is separate from humans, animals, and inanimate objects.

IT'S ALL *the* SAME *to* ME

Raymond Buckland's words reflect the philosophy of *monism*, which is defined as "the view that reality is one unitary organic whole with no independant parts." In other words, all things are believed to possess one spirit or be part of a universal whole.

According to the book of Genesis, God chose to create men and women in His image:

> God created man in his own image, in the image of God he created him; male and female he created them.
>
> God blessed them and said to them, "Be fruitful and increase in number; fill the earth and subdue it. Rule over the fish of the sea and the birds of the air and over every living creature that moves on the ground" (Genesis 1:27-28).

God reigns supreme over the heavens and the earth. Psalm 22:28 reminds us that "dominion belongs to the LORD and he rules over the nations." Yet, when God created humans, He also established a system in which humans would preside over His creation and care for it.

Monism teaches that the reason problems exist in the world today is because of ignorance rather than evil. It asserts that if people truly understood and accepted that we are all interconnected with each other and the universe, then no harm or evil would ever occur.

We don't have to live for long in this world, though, to discover from personal experience that evil abounds. Clearly, Satan is alive and well, and he has convinced millions of people to believe his lies. This is not surprising, since his name is literally translated "accuser," "deceiver," or "adversary" (enemy).

We're called to arm ourselves against this deceiver, Satan. The apostle Peter warns us, "Be self-controlled and alert. Your enemy the devil prowls around like a roaring lion looking for someone to devour" (1 Peter 5:8). We also have to be aware that "Satan himself masquerades as an angel of light" (2 Corinthians 11:14). Since the beginning, Satan has misled people by mimicking and counterfeiting God as closely as he can.

Thankfully, our God is all powerful—infinitely more powerful than Satan. But how can we, in our sinful state, ever relate to such a holy, mighty, and awesome God? He made a way by sending His Son, Jesus, to earth. Jesus emptied Himself of glory to clothe Himself in the humble flesh of humanity and to live on earth as a man. He was fully man, yet also fully God. Jesus lived, died, and rose from the dead to demonstrate His power over the grave and to redeem us from our sins.

When we choose to place our faith in Christ, the Bible says that the Holy Spirit, the third Person of the Trinity, immediately comes to dwell in our hearts. John 14:26 says, "The Counselor, the Holy Spirit, whom the Father will send in my name, will teach you all things and will remind you of everything I have said to you." In this way, God does reside within us. However, the Holy Spirit dwells only within people; He does not indwell animals or inanimate objects.

"God Is Everything"

Another common philosophy, pantheism, teaches that God is Everything, and Everything is God. According to this worldview, everything in creation is a part of God. This includes the sun, the moon, trees, turtles, and rocks; everything has a divine nature. Julia Phillips and Matthew Sandow state, "To a Wiccan, all of creation is divine, and by realizing how we are connected to the turning of the seasons and to the natural world, we come to a deeper understanding to the ways in which we are connected to the God and Goddess."[3]

Pantheism takes the loving, personal God of the Bible and converts Him into an impersonal force. It suggests that if we are part of God, then we can't be sinful, and therefore, we have no need for a Savior. Principles like these can lead people to worship creation rather than the Creator—which is specifically forbidden in Scripture, according to the book of Romans:

> Since the creation of the world God's invisible qualities—his eternal power and divine nature—have been clearly seen, being understood from what has been made, so that men are without excuse.
>
> For although they knew God, they neither glorified him as God nor gave thanks to him, but their thinking became futile and their foolish hearts were darkened. Although they claimed to be wise, they became fools and exchanged the glory of the immortal God for images made to look like mortal man and birds and animals and reptiles.
>
> Therefore God gave them over in the sinful desires of their hearts to sexual impurity for the degrading of their bodies with one another. They exchanged the truth of God for a lie, and worshiped and served created things rather than the Creator—who is forever praised. Amen (Romans 1:20-25).

Ecology is one of Wicca's most revered tenets because Wiccans envision the earth as a living goddess who blesses her people with her abundance. In return, Wiccans believe that this planet's inhabitants should care for Mother Earth and work hard to protect her limited and precious resources.

As Christians, we believe that God gave His people dominion over the earth—and that many of us have not done our part in preserving and protecting it. God granted us this magnificent gift, expecting us to be conscientious caretakers—*not* expecting us to destroy it and sap all of its resources. Personal sacrifices may be required at times in order for us to honor our call to be wise stewards of the earth. Our children and grandchildren's welfare will depend partly on what we do *right now* to preserve the environment.

The Wheel of the Year

"O do not tell the Priests of our art, for they would call it sin; but we've been out in the woods all night, a conjurin' summer in..."

—Rudyard Kipling[4]

When I (Marla) contacted a Wiccan association for information about Wicca's commitment to caring for the environment, a high priestess named Sarah (not her real name) e-mailed me back almost immediately. She kindly and graciously answered my questions about Wicca and invited me to attend a full-moon ritual as part of the celebration of the Wheel of the Year.

When I asked Sarah how she became a Wiccan, she wrote,

> I am a Witch and have always been a Witch, just finding out that Wicca was very much involved in the magick of nature, symbols, and synchronization of everything around us, made me more interested and in tune with my surroundings. However, on a different note, I also encountered problems and false promises in Christianity. This, my friend, is a very long story which is one of the subjects we usually discuss in our circle after our rituals. There is so much to learn in the beautiful religion of Wicca, for it is celebrated as a nature and fertility-based religion for all and is usually very comfortable for most.[5]

As we mentioned in chapter 5, the Wheel of the Year—the Wiccan sacred calendar—is marked by eight festivals that celebrate the eternal cycle of life, reflected in the changing of the seasons and the cycles of birth, maturation, death, and resurrection. The Wheel of the Year bears great significance to Wiccans and provides a vital key to understanding the religion:

By following the Wiccan religion you are affirming your belief in the sanctity of the Earth, and acknowledging that you depend upon the Earth for your very life. Although modern lifestyles do not encourage awareness of our personal relationship with the turning seasons, or the patterns of life, growth, death and decay, that does not mean that they no longer exist. The ebb and flow of the Earth's energies may be hidden beneath a physical shell of tarmac and concrete, and a psychic one of human indifference, but they are nevertheless there for those who wish to acknowledge them once more.[6]

A YEARLY CELEBRATION

The "witchy" mystique of Salem, Massachusetts, never died. Rather, the Salem witch hunts planted a kernel of intrigue in people's minds and hearts that continued to blossom, and the inhabitants of this once-tiny village have capitalized on its reputation as "the witchcraft capital of America." Now, thousands of people flock there every year to celebrate Halloween and to learn more about witchcraft.

One Salem business owner said that the Halloween season there is a monthlong celebration with a tremendous impact on the local economy and culture. He couldn't imagine Salem without its notoriety as the birthplace of American witchcraft.

The Reclaiming Movement

Many Wiccans have chosen to join an earth-based movement called Reclaiming—a community of Wiccan women and men, first established in San Francisco, who work together to unify spirit and politics. According to Reclaiming's website, its vision is rooted in the religion and magick of "the Goddess, the Immanent Life Force." Members of the Reclaiming movement view their work as teaching and making magick; the art of empowering themselves and each other. They use their skills to deepen their strength, both as individuals and as a community, to voice their concerns about the world they live in, and to birth a vision of a new culture.[7] As with the Wiccan religion itself, most of the adherents of Reclaiming are female.

Reclaiming hosts a wide variety of community events, including a biennial Dandelion Gathering held in the spring. The theme of the 2008 Dandelion Gathering was *All the Infinite Possibilities*, accompanied by the following credo:

> *We come to celebrate our communities,*
> *The Seen and the Unseen,*
> *To remember our lineage,*
> *To strengthen our resolve to serve all beings.*

Reclaiming also holds WitchCamps—intensive retreats held in a campground setting for the study of magick and ritual. WitchCamps are open to men and women at all levels of experience, allowing newcomers to learn the basic skills of magick and ritual. Advanced paths offer the chance to apply the tools of ritual to personal healing and empowerment.[8]

Starhawk, one of Wicca's most revered teachers and authors, established the Reclaiming movement. She provides an excellent explanation of it:

> Reclaiming is a tradition of the Craft...Our style of ritual could be described with the acronym EIEIO:
>
> + Ecstatic: ...We aim to create a high intensity of energy that is passionate and pleasurable.
>
> + Improvisational: We value spontaneity within the overall structure of our rituals.
>
> + Ensemble: In our larger group rituals, we work with many priest/esses together taking different roles and performing different functions that, ideally, support each other like the members of a good jazz ensemble.
>
> + Inspired: Because we each have access to the sacred, we are each capable of creating elements of ritual...We are

not bound by the past, for divine inspiration is constantly present in each of us.

+ Organic: We strive for a smooth, coherent flow of energy...Our rituals are linked to the rhythms of cyclical time and organic life.

We honor the community-building work of organizing, bookkeeping, phone-calling, e-mailing, Xeroxing, gardening, cooking, cleaning, building, fixing, childrearing, and all the behind-the-scenes tasks of ritual making. Our organizational structures must reflect our core values just as our rituals do. We respect authentic leadership and expertise, but we encourage the sharing and rotation of roles and responsibilities. We do not institute hierarchies of power. We make decisions by consensus, as the process most in keeping with our recognition of the sacred within each individual. We strive to treat each other with honesty, caring and respect.[9]

Reclaiming allows Wiccans to feel a sense of responsibility and community as they care for the earth, and it also enables them to meld their religious and political principles into a harmonious whole and to dialogue with others who share the same faith. Movements such as Reclaiming provide a compelling impetus for men and women to follow Wicca.

Spiral Scouts

As we mentioned in chapter 1, Wiccan parents now have the option of enrolling their children and teens in Spiral Scouts—"the pagan answer to Boy Scouts and Girl Scouts."[10] This international organization allows children of pagan and other minority faiths to participate in activities that emphasize ecology as well as the teaching of mythology and the telling of traditional stories. It's open to boys and girls of a broad range of pagan faiths, not just Wicca. Unlike other scouting programs, Spiral Scouts emphasizes that membership is open to all children, including gays and lesbians and children with gay and lesbian parents.[11]

My Own Green Journey

After exploring Wiccans' commitment to preserving the earth and conserving its limited natural resources, my husband and I (Marla) felt motivated to examine our attitudes toward the environment—and to analyze the carbon footprint we've been leaving. The skyrocketing prices of fuel and other natural resources also have caused us to be more aware of our levels of consumption.

Since I began the research for this book, we've made an effort to recycle and to conserve electricity and water. I work from home as a full-time author, so I drive less than I once did. I combine errands to save fuel. In addition, my husband works from his home office on certain days. This helps us save money on fuel and tolls, as well as cutting down on our environmental emissions.

I also like to "go green" by getting outside and enjoying nature. I love interacting with people, and I also love being outside. Clearly, this can be a challenge for someone with a career as a writer! To maintain spiritual and emotional balance in my life, I spend at least a few hours each day away from my desk, enjoying nature and exercising.

I gain most of my writing inspiration while I'm spending time in a natural environment. It saddens me to see the open fields and beautiful trees in our area dwindle as hotels, restaurants, cookie-cutter housing developments, parking lots, and office buildings spring up all around us.

Scripture tells us, "The heavens declare the glory of God; the skies proclaim the work of his hands" (Psalm 19:1). Yet many of us spend little more than a few minutes outside each day. Some people stay outdoors only for the time it takes them to get into their car in the morning and then back into their house at night. Taking at least 30 minutes every day to rediscover the beauty and the peaceful calm of nature would do us all good. Exploring God's creation reminds us of His extraordinary love for us.

In Part Two of *Generation Hex*, we'll move from answering the question "What is Wicca?" to discussing some of the ways you can reach out to Wicca's practitioners. Read on; your journey has just begun!

Part Two

WHAT SHOULD
I DO ABOUT WICCA?

"Mom, Today Someone Cast a Spell on Me!"

Wicca and Today's Teenagers

"I've been putting together a series of news pieces on how young people in the States practice their various faiths, and I'd like to include a segment on Wicca. It seems to me to be a growing faith that is often misunderstood because of sensationalistic portrayals in the media."

—ALEX MAR, ON HIS INTEREST ABOUT
A SEGMENT ON WICCA FOR MTV[1]

In my research on Wicca among today's teenagers, I (Dillon) came across the following article from FamilyEducation.com that reveals the attitude of a teenager involved in Wicca:

> "I'm very proud of what I am," says 21-year-old Angelique T. She identifies herself as a witch and practices Wicca, a naturalistic pagan religion that dates back to the time of the Druids in ancient Europe. "If I have a problem at work, which I do right now, my favorite thing to do is to burn a white candle and ask the goddess for whatever it is that I need."
>
> Angelique's mother, an author who goes by the pen name Silver RavenWolf, has written *Teen Witch: Wicca for a New Generation* (Llewellyn Publications). RavenWolf's publishers say the book is one of their fastest sellers, testament to Wicca's growing appeal to teenagers.

"Most of the letters I get are from kids who want to be more spiritual," RavenWolf offers. "In a world where (teens) are perceived to have little control, I would think Wicca would be self-empowering. You don't have to rely on others to tell you what God said. You can speak to God in your own way."[2]

The book *Teen Witch* has sold at least 150,000 copies, according to reports from its publisher, creating a new niche market of books on witchcraft targeted toward a teen audience. But who is reading these books? Catherine Edwards Sanders, in her excellent book *Wicca's Charm*, shares the following challenge:

> Conduct the following survey and consider the results; they might surprise you. Five years ago they surprised me. Find a group of seventeen-year-old girls in private and public schools, in red states or blue, and ask if any of them have Wiccan friends or know people interested in Wicca. When I asked a group of teenagers at my church this question, all the girls raised their hands.[3]

In my informal discussions, I've noticed a disturbing trend. When I ask teenagers if they know anyone who is into Wicca or witchcraft, the answer is nearly always a unanimous "yes." But when I ask youth pastors, church leaders, or parents if they know anyone involved in Wicca or witchcraft, the vast majority give me a blank stare. Clearly, there's a disconnect between what is happening with teenagers' involvement in Wicca and what church leaders and parents *think* is happening.

In this chapter, we'll share some of the trends in today's youth culture regarding Wicca, current harmful attitudes toward teenagers involved in the craft, and some suggestions on how to discuss concerns about Wicca or witchcraft with your teenage son, daughter, or friend.

Teenage Involvement in Wicca

One Wiccan practitioner named Michael, a high school senior from Missouri, told me his story about his involvement with the craft. In addition to serving as a practitioner, he has formed an online discussion group for what he calls "Christian Wicca," a blending of faiths he believes provides a more accurate picture of both Wicca and Christianity. His story highlights the attempts by a growing number of people to integrate Wiccan beliefs with their Christian perspective:

> My story is one that is short-lived at this time, as I am a practitioner of only a few months. I was born into a practically atheist home and found Christianity at the age of 14. I began to question my faith and denounced Christianity and started studying some other religions. I have not been able to go too far at this time due to a lack of funds and a good library. But I started studying the book *Earth Power* (Scott Cunningham), and started to dabble in some of its practices and a few others. I purchased *The Craft* (Dorothy Morrison) and *Wicca: A Guide for the Solitary Practitioner* (Cunningham) and found myself in a faith I could truly hold dear to my heart.
>
> I did, however, feel somewhat empty still. Jesus has been a part of my life for almost three years, and has helped me become who I am today. I started looking into Christian Wicca then.
>
> I follow the Wiccan Rede, but also take the Ten Commandments to heart greatly. "You shall not hold any Gods before me." This is one that people really don't get when it comes to my beliefs. I believe that there is only One true God, and that all other gods are part of the One. The Christian Trinity (Father, Son, and Holy Spirit) is also somewhat of a reflection of this. I view it as God, Goddess (the feminine quality of God), and Jesus, all still being part of One being.

Though Michael's beliefs are distinctly different from my own, I appreciated his honesty and openness. But his story is not as uncommon as we might think.

Unfortunately, Christians and some non-Christians have responded in ways that have made the situation worse. One former Wiccan I interviewed told me that during high school a guy came up to her on the street, shook her, and yelled at her that she was going to hell. And Jessica, one of the Wiccans that Marla interviewed, said that people at her high school would shout, "You shall not suffer a witch to live!" as she walked down the hall. Clearly, inside today's schools and classrooms, some teenagers have experienced serious mistreatment for their affiliation with Wicca.

Discrimination Against Teenage Wiccans

Since 1998, at least nine lawsuits have been filed regarding Wiccan pentacles being worn in schools.[4] Children as young as 12 years old have been banned from wearing necklaces or earrings bearing pentacles or pentagrams to school, with administrators stating that this jewelry was "unapproved school attire."

However, such situations are beginning to change. A Dallas–Fort Worth TV station, NBC5, conducted an opinion poll over a Waxahachie, Texas, case in August 2002. Of those who voted, 77 percent were in favor of students being allowed to wear a pentacle or pentagram to school.[5]

IT'S ALL ON *the* INTERNET

Your teenager can register for classes at WitchSchool.com to become certified in Living the Wiccan Life and Correllian Wicca for a nominal fee of $30.

For Christians, this can be a topic of conflict. Parents desire to keep their children from being exposed to what they consider an offensive religious symbol. However, the rules that would prevent Wiccans from wearing a pentacle or pentagram around their necks could just as easily be used to keep Christians from wearing cross necklaces to school or holding Christmas parties. In all fairness, the pentacle is a religious symbol important to many Wiccans in the same way that the cross is important to us.

Sometimes Wiccan teens experience threats or even physical intimidation. "One time (in high school) my mother had to get involved because a boy was slamming my wrists and my kneecaps into my locker," recalls Angelique T. "We also had a pottery wheel in art, and you would need to put your name on a calendar to sign up to use it. And this boy would write 'Satan' underneath my name."[6]

In addition, parents have fiercely protested the practice of Wicca or witchcraft by their own children. Jessica, the Wiccan teen mentioned earlier, said, "Wicca is not a parent-friendly religion." While this is understandable, some parents have reacted so negatively to their teen's interest in Wicca that their teenage daughter or son has resorted to practicing the craft secretly.

One further source of discrimination that sometimes occurs is toward children or teenagers whose *parents* are involved in the craft. One anonymous Wiccan mother from Virginia said, "I would love to be able to say 'Accept us for who we are,' but I can't, mainly because of my kids...Children can be cruel, and their parents can be even more cruel, and I don't want my kids picked on for the choice their mommy made."[7]

Talking to Teenagers About Involvement in Witchcraft

As a parent, youth worker, or other person involved in the life of a teenager who practices Wicca, what can you do? How can you help? Should you intervene? We don't claim to know all the answers, but here are some of the guidelines we have gathered from our discussions with teenagers involved in the craft.

Hear Them Out

If you're a parent who has recently discovered that your teen is involved in Wicca, you may want to yell, scream, or cry, but that's not likely to help. If your kid thinks you don't care enough to listen to him or her, why would he or she be interested in the alternatives you suggest? As hard as it may be to listen, respect your teenager enough to at least hear his or her side of the story.

Take Appropriate Action

As a parent, you have the authority to tell your teenager that you will not allow him or her to practice witchcraft in any form in your home. Again, the *way* you say this is as important as *what* you say, but you can lovingly request that all items associated with witchcraft be removed from your home and practices ended.

While some of the Wiccans we interviewed might be upset at this response, you as a parent are the primary spiritual influence on your teenager. This means that if you tell your teen that Wicca or witchcraft is not okay, then you need to explain what forms of spirituality are acceptable for your family. If you are a Christian, you'll need resources such as the Bible and this book to help provide understanding of why you disagree with your teenager's view.

Even some Wiccan writers agree that teenagers must follow the leadership of their parents regarding involvement in Wicca. Patti Wigington, who has studied Wicca for over 20 years, writes,

> In some cases, parents may strongly object to their child's practicing Wicca or Paganism. This is usually because of the teachings of their religious beliefs—and as parents, that is their right. They are entitled to tell their child that he or she is not allowed to practice Wicca, belong to a coven, or even own books about the subject. If this is the case in your family, there are a number of things you can do.[8]

The convicting part of this scenario is that your teenager may have chosen Wicca because he or she was not finding spiritual fulfillment in your home or church. As your teen's spiritual leader, you are now being challenged to offer something that is better than what he or she is experiencing in witchcraft. Biblical Christianity does offer a better and more powerful alternative, but you have to live it out with integrity in order for your teenager to see it.

TO LOVE *and* PROTECT

For parents and youth workers, services are available through Covenant Eyes (www.covenanteyes.com) for monitoring your child or teenager's web surfing activities. See the organization's website for more information.

Keep a Long-Term Perspective

When we say long-term, we mean really long—an *eternal* perspective. Your goal as a parent or youth worker is not just to win an argument. Your role is to point the way to the true and living God. Your teenager may become angry at any requirements for change you make, but don't let this discourage you. Your goal is to make the best long-term decisions possible to help your teenager follow Jesus Christ.

We've included some online responses to the question, "Do your parents know you are involved in Wicca?" Our hope is that you'll be sensitive to your teen's concerns and use these examples to help you respond in a way that is both Christ-honoring and compassionate.

> I am posting this because my parents don't know I'm Wiccan, and I know a few people that keep it from everyone, apart from their closest friends or other Wiccans. I don't tell my parents because they don't need to know, and I wouldn't want them to jump to conclusions about it and judge it now. I may tell them in the future and I may tell everyone I meet in the future about it, but for now I am fine as I am.

> With my allowance I got two Pagan books, but when my mother saw my choices in my hand in the checkout line she freaked, saying if I wanted to spend my money on that [junk] I will have no more allowance. Still, I know I have it better than a lot of people. A couple of months ago I was speaking with a Christian mother on ICQ and she informed me if her child ever strayed from Jesus, she would

kill him. At least he would be in heaven and not sinning, and she would join him one day, she said. At first I thought she wasn't serious, but I was wrong. A shiver went down my back thinking of her as my mother, and I realized even though I don't have it easy, it can always get worse, and I was thankful for what I had.[9]

Many teenagers experience tremendous conflict with their parents over their involvement in witchcraft. These examples may seem extreme, but they reveal some of the legitimate concerns of teenagers involved in Wicca today.

But what happens when these teenagers leave home for their college campuses? With newfound freedom and like-minded friends, "coming out of the broom closet" has become a new way of life for many college students. In the following chapter, we'll explore the ways Wicca is taking root on campuses in the U.S. and worldwide.

"My Roommate Is a Witch...Really!"

Wicca on America's College Campuses

*"Witches and 'neo-pagans' are a fixture on
many American college campuses."*
—PETER WOOD, ASSOCIATE PROVOST, BOSTON COLLEGE[1]

In gathering information for this chapter, I (Dillon) discovered a
Wicca group on Facebook, a leading online social networking site.
One of the group's moderators, who goes by the craft name Ariawn,
is a 23-year-old recent graduate from a Midwestern university. She
described to me the role Facebook has played in connecting her with
other Wiccans:

> Facebook has helped me in many ways to connect with
> other people. I met another girl on Facebook who was
> Wiccan and went to my school, which was Catholic. I
> also met a current student of mine, to whom I teach my
> Wiccan tradition, about a year ago on Facebook, and he's
> about to undergo evaluation for his first-degree initiation.
> I also met one boyfriend who was not Wiccan but a Pagan
> nonetheless. Sadly, he and I have since parted ways, but we
> learned a lot from each other about devotion to our gods.
> Most importantly, however, Facebook has given me a direct
> link to people who actually practice a myriad of Pagan and
> Wiccan paths, and I can go straight to a primary source
> for information and have it checked and cross-checked in a
> short period of time.

I also asked Ariawn about the people who are involved in the craft.

> Young people…college students…make up a good-sized
> bulk of it. I also find that a lot of fringe people are attracted
> to this path…the especially ugly, especially beautiful, espe-
> cially rich, especially poor, especially intelligent, those who
> suffer from psychiatric problems. People from all walks of
> life follow this path. I know one man who as of five years
> ago was homeless, but Wicca helped him to turn his life
> around…and then there is Sully Erna of Godsmack, who
> is fairly public about being Wiccan. Myself, I want to be
> a doctor, whereas my High Priest was a Navy man and
> now works in an office for a heating and air-conditioning
> company.

Few people realize that over a hundred major U.S. college campuses include officially recognized pagan organizations. Pagans
on Campus[2] and CollegeWicca.com help student organizations
exchange information and make connections among their growing
members. Harvard University's Pluralism Project website includes
links to more than a hundred recognized neopagan college groups
as well.[3]

AND *the* ARMED FORCES

Many young (and some not-so-young) adults openly practice Wicca
within the U.S. military, where it has been a legally recognized religion since 1986. According to a 2006 *Washington Post* report, the
Pentagon lists 1800 self-reported Wiccans on active duty in the
armed forces.[7] See chapter 12 for more on this issue.

Green Spiral, the name of Michigan State University's student
organization representing the "eclectic pagan network," includes links
to upcoming tarot card classes, a local coven, and recommendations
for various pagan and witchcraft reading materials.[4]

Many major U.S. campuses also offer regular college courses on various aspects of Wicca, witchcraft, or neopaganism. Circle Sanctuary, a nonprofit organization dedicated to research, spiritual healing, community celebrations, and education, provides a Pagan Academic Network to facilitate communication and information sharing among academic leaders in paganism.[5] Due to its growing expertise, the Circle Sanctuary's efforts have been highlighted in various U.S. news media and on the BBC.[6]

Media Highlights and Coverage

Many college students and young adults, especially women, have been drawn to Wicca by the romanticized view of witchcraft in today's media. Jami Shoemaker, a publicist for Wiccan publisher Llewellyn, told the *New York Times*, "The contemporary witch is the beautiful 25-year-old that you see on TV."[8] Popular TV shows and movies such as *Charmed* and *Buffy the Vampire Slayer* have downplayed the darkness and dangers of witchcraft and have instead made it seem flashy, fun, and exciting.

The following list details some of the recent media that have promoted witchcraft among college students and young adults:

+ *Angel*, TV show
+ *Bell Witch*, 2007 movie
+ *Bewitched*, TV show and 2005 movie
+ *The Blair Witch Project*, 1999 movie
+ *Book of Shadows: Blair Witch 2*, 2000 movie
+ *Buffy the Vampire Slayer*, TV show
+ *The Craft*, 1996 movie
+ *Hocus Pocus*, 1993 movie
+ *Practical Magic*, 1998 movie
+ *Sabrina the Teenage Witch*, TV show

College students seek a religion that's authentic and extreme—one that makes them feel empowered, with a strong message and high-impact visuals. They get that with Wicca.

Wicca on Campus

Some pagan student organizations can request university funds just like any other student organization. On other campuses, such as Lehigh University in Pennsylvania and the University of Arizona, students can be excused from classes on Wiccan holidays.

As we mentioned earlier, in addition to university policy shifts, a growing number of campuses also include coursework on witchcraft, Wicca, or paganism. The following course listings are only a small sampling:

+ "History of European Witchcraft," College of Oneonta, New York
+ "The Science of Harry Potter," Frostburg State University, Maryland
+ "Witchcraft and Politics," Bucknell University, Pennsylvania
+ "History of Witchcraft and Magic," Syracuse University, New York

Majors in women's spirituality, along with humanities programs with a growing focus on paganism and Wiccan traditions, have provided opportunities for interested college students to learn more about Wicca and perform research on Wiccan religious traditions.

Why the Attraction?

Why are college students some of the most likely people to get involved in Wicca? One reason is the freedom of college life. When Mom and Dad are not around to say no, there are new opportunities to experiment and find one's own spiritual path.

A second reason college students are attracted to Wicca is the sense of community. College students often live in new locations far from family and high school friends, and they long to connect in authentic relationships. If a roommate or classmate is into Wicca and happens to be the friendliest person around, why not try Wicca?

Another attraction for college students is Wicca's focus on environmentalism. As a nature-based religion, Wiccan practitioners are often highly involved in promoting environmental issues on campus. Through this involvement, those in the craft connect with other students who care about the environment, providing a natural platform for discussing values in other areas of life.

Wicca also attracts some female college students due to its heightened focus on the value and spiritual contribution of women. If they begin to believe that God is both male and female, women start to feel confident that their involvement in Wicca will make them feel valued rather than minimized.

Further, the online relationships and sharing of information have made it easier for those interested in Wicca to connect on campus. Many campuses, such as my alma mater (Indiana State University), include laptop computers for every freshman student. Most announcements are now made via e-mail on campus computers rather than through flyers on bulletin boards.

One major reason college students are attracted to Wicca is its promise of spiritual power. Christianity is perceived as a life of rules and regulations. Wicca is seen as a spiritual path that enables people to connect with the supernatural and harness the earth's energy.

What Do College Wiccans Do?

It's easy in some ways to understand why Wicca appeals to college students, but what do college Wiccans do? You might be surprised that in many cases, their activities mirror those of any other religious group, including Christian campus organizations.

At Colorado State University, the Pagan Student Association (which includes both Wiccans and those of other pagan traditions) promotes its group through the yearly Centertainment showcase, along with a hundred other groups on campus. Each spring, the group participates alongside other campus groups in service projects to assist residents across their community.[9] Many campus groups have also given to humanitarian causes such as Hurricane Katrina and tsunami disaster relief.

In addition to these public signs of goodwill, many pagan student organizations meet regularly to discuss various aspects of witchcraft and paganism. At other times, groups gather to celebrate Wiccan holidays. At the University of Maine-Orono, the Pagan Campus Organization website includes pictures from the group's Beltane bonfire and provides meeting opportunities to celebrate full moon rituals.[10] At the University of Syracuse, students from the Pagan Student Society have set up lighted candles in the campus chapel.[11]

As a result of this combination of community service, close-knit relationships, concern for nature, and personal spiritual focus, a small but growing number of college students are becoming involved in Wicca.

Students as Solitary Practitioners

In addition to over 100 student organizations devoted to this area of life on campuses across the nation, many more people commit their time to Wicca as solitary practitioners. This simply means they practice their religion personally, but do not meet with others who do.

ALONE ON CAMPUS

Fox News reports that Elizabeth (who didn't want her last name used), a 24-year-old Georgetown University graduate who was raised Catholic, hasn't told her parents she's a practicing Wiccan, and told few people at school about her faith. "I pretty much practiced as a solitary the entire time I was there," she said.[12]

No one really knows how many people practice solitary Wicca, but it's safe to say that many college students beyond those who meet in school-sanctioned organizations seek information about pagan traditions for their personal practices.

Ariawn, mentioned at the beginning of this chapter, also shared some of the trends she's spotted regarding involvement in Wicca. "I've seen a lot of activity from Canada, especially British Columbia, Australia, and the United Kingdom, England specifically." Yet, in her words, "My Facebook group is way too big to really get a feel for what areas of the world are most active." As of the time of our interview, her Facebook group had over 5700 members from all around the world, most of whom are college-age and who spend their time connecting, talking about, and learning more about the traditions of Wicca and paganism.

In the following chapter, we'll discuss Wicca's growing popularity among members of the U.S. military.

Emblems of Belief

Wicca in the U.S. Military

*"We provide for freedom of religion in the military.
That's why we put the uniform on every day."*
—COL. W. RANDY ROBNETT,
WING CHAPLAIN, TRAVIS AIR FORCE BASE[1]

The night wind pushed Don Larsen's green robe against his lanky frame. A circle of torches lit his face.

"The old gods are standing near!" called a retired army intelligence officer.

"To watch the turning of the year!" replied the wife of a soldier wounded in Iraq.

"What night is this?" called a former fighter pilot.

"It is the night of Imbolc!" responded Larsen, a former army chaplain.

Sixteen self-described witches gathered on a Texas plain to celebrate Imbolc, a late-winter pagan festival, with dancing, chanting, chili, and beer. All but two were current or former military personnel. And all of them had stories—personal journeys that led them away from Christianity and convinced them to embrace Wicca.

On July 6, 2006, Don Larsen applied to become the first Wiccan chaplain in the U.S. armed forces. According to an article in the *Washington Post*, Larsen's superiors not only denied his request but also withdrew him from Iraq and removed him from the chaplain corps, despite an unblemished service record.[2]

Larsen's story, in addition to multiple protests and lawsuits brought by Wiccans, put pressure on the military to change its tactics. Selena Fox, a Wiccan high priestess, psychotherapist, and the founder of Circle Sanctuary, a 200-acre nature center in Mt. Horeb, Wisconsin, fought on the frontlines of the legal battle to have the Wiccan pentacle engraved on the headstones of military veterans.

The remains of two U.S. soldiers are buried at Circle Sanctuary's cemetery: a Vietnam veteran from Ohio and Jerome Birnbaum, a Korean War veteran. The cemetery also holds a memorial for National Guard Sgt. Patrick Stewart, who was killed in Afghanistan in 2005. Stewart and Birnbaum's widows sued for the right to have the Wiccan pentacle engraved on their husbands' burial stones.[3] Their petition was granted when the U.S. Department of Veterans Affairs settled the lawsuit in April 2007 by agreeing to add the Wiccan pentacle to gravestones.

What Resources Are Available for Military Wiccans?

The U.S. military operates a Military Pagan Network to provide support and resources for Wiccans. According to its website, the mission of the Military Pagan Network is to

+ advocate for those faced with harassment or discrimination
+ facilitate networking within the military Pagan community
+ provide information to military and government agencies regarding various Neopagan practices
+ suggest to military and government agencies additions or modifications to regulations and policies that will both include and take into consideration Neopagan religions and practices[4]

The Military Pagan Network also provides a glossary of the various types of pagan belief systems and practices that it protects:

+ *Mesopaganism:* Describes religions founded as attempts to recreate, revive or continue what their founders thought of as the Paleopagan ways of their ancestors (or predecessors), but which were heavily influenced (accidentally, deliberately and/or involuntarily) by the monotheistic and dualistic worldviews of Judaism, Christianity and/or Islam. Examples of Mesopagan belief systems include Freemasonry, Rosicrucianism, Theosophy, Spiritualism, Druidism as practiced by the Masonic-influenced fraternal movements in Europe and the Celtic Isles, the many Afro-Diasporatic faiths (such as Voudoun, Santeria, Macumba, and so on).

+ *Neopaganism:* A collection of diverse contemporary religions rooted in indigenous traditions or deriving inspiration therefrom, characterized by a belief in the interconnection of all life, personal autonomy, and immanent divinities. Often nature-centered and supportive of gender equity.

+ *Pagan:* Any person who belongs to a Neopagan or Paleopagan religion. Not generally used by those who are part of a Mesopagan religious group.

+ *Paganism:* An umbrella term that covers Neopaganism, Mesopaganism and Paleopaganism.

+ *Paleopaganism:* Refers to the original tribal faiths of Europe, Africa, Asia, the Americas, Oceania and Australia, when they were (or in some cases, still are) practiced as intact belief systems. Of the so-called "Great Religions of the World," Hinduism (prior to the influx of Islam into India), Taoism and Shinto, for example, fall under this category.

+ *Occultist:* Any person who belongs to a Mesopagan religious group. Examples are members of the OTO and the Golden Dawn.[5]

According to Wicca.com, Wiccans in the military

> range from career military personnel to conscientious objectors. Wiccans do not proselytize and generally resent those

who do. They believe that no one Path to the Sacred is right for all people, and see their own religious pattern as only one among many that are equally worthy. Wiccans respect all religions that foster honor and compassion in their adherents, and expect the same respect. Members are encouraged to learn about all faiths, and are permitted to attend the services of other religions, should they desire to do so.[6]

How Many Wiccans Are in the Military?

According to 2005 Defense Department statistics, about 1800 active-duty service members identified themselves as Wiccans at that time.[7] Something about Wicca clearly fills a niche for soldiers searching for meaningful faith.

Wiccans exist in all military branches, and some in the top ranks. By the Pentagon's count, there are now over 1500 self-identified Wiccans in the air force and over 350 in the marines. No exact figures are available for the much larger army and navy. Wiccan groups estimate they have at least 4000 followers in uniform, but they say many active-duty Wiccans hide their beliefs to avoid ridicule and discrimination.[8]

After U.S. military personnel pelted American Wiccan servicemen and servicewomen in Iraq with bottles and rocks as they worshipped in a sacred circle, the Pentagon turned to a chaplain named Patrick McCollum to "conjure a little Wicca 101 for the troops." Problems had arisen among Wiccans in the military because some chaplains were trying to convert them, and their commanding officers would not allow them to practice their rituals.[9]

Many military bases now have Wiccan circles and hold pagan religious services. In addition, soldiers may have their dog tags engraved to identify them as Wiccans.[10] Surprisingly, since 1978 the Army Chaplain handbook has listed ways to accommodate Wiccans.

What Are the Concerns of Wiccans in the Military?

Many Wiccans in the U.S. armed forces keep their religion under wraps for fear of discrimination and persecution. At the start of a recent readiness run, a chaplain prayed in the name of the heavenly Father. "That's where it gets awkward with me," said Wiccan Staff Sergeant Katie McDaniel. "We're at a military function and there are prayers. I don't mind the words of inspiration, as they call it these days, as long as it's nondenominational, as long as it doesn't call on particular deities."[11]

Another Wiccan writes, "Another problem that has become a blight on the Pagan-Military community is how some Pagans use their 'religious' beliefs to attempt to get out of going to combat. This makes other Pagans throughout the Armed Forces look bad and also gives people the wrong impression of us all. One bad apple does not spoil the whole bunch, but it does make us look bad."[12]

The Reverend Darius Morningstar serves in the U.S. Air Force as a language specialist at Fort Meade. Not only have his colleagues been tolerant of his faith, he says, but policy changes have made the military more friendly to Wiccans.

Wiccans now have the freedom to worship openly on military bases. A controversy arose in the late 1990s at Fort Hood in Texas, where many local Christians objected to Wiccan activity. But the Defense Department said Wiccans, as members of a government-recognized religion, had the right to practice their faith on the base. "My faith is not so distant from all the others," Morningstar said. "We all create our own deity as a gateway to the divine."[13]

Another Wiccan soldier explains how he came to follow Wicca:

> My very good and close friend told me I was ready to see something another way, and she brought me to a weekend Gathering. That was the first day of the rest of my life. It felt as if I could finally breathe. I was alive in the woods and surrounded by amazing people...Since then I have felt more in touch with myself and the world, things make more sense, [and] I feel an energy inside.[14]

I (Marla) support the right of Wiccans to practice their religion, and I'm filled with gratitude to our troops for putting their lives on the line every day to provide us with the freedom and safety we enjoy. But still, I'm saddened to see so many people turning away from their Christian faith or choosing Wicca instead of Christianity. The stress of rigorous physical training, the pain of being separated from loved ones, and the mental and emotional trauma of warfare can cause many people to have a crisis of faith. Yet during battle and while enduring those "dark seasons of the night," these soldiers need God more than ever.

I've always sought to turn away from violence. War is an ugly thing; its raw power, horrific situations, and mind-searing images make people desire peace as well as a faith that is powerful, real, and tangible—stronger than any enemy they may face. Those who enter the military with a lukewarm faith often find that faith lacking when they encounter the battles and trenches of a foreign land.

AN OPPORTUNITY *to* INTERCEDE

When was the last time you prayed for America's soldiers? Take a few minutes to do it now. In addition to your prayers for protection, pray that God will protect the faith of those who are Christians and that He will move them to share His truth with those around them. Also pray for Christian military chaplains to have wisdom in sharing the gospel with service people of all faiths.

A Journal Entry from a Pagan Soldier

The following journal entry provides you with a first-person perspective of what it's like to be a pagan in the military.

> Here I am, on twenty-four-hour duty, in Baghdad, Iraq. Yes, I'm a soldier, and I'm proud to be Pagan. I am the current Distinctive Faith Group Leader (DFGL) for the Victory Base Open Circle (VBOC). (It is a bad habit in the military to make everything into an acronym.) What that means is that I do the administrative work to keep

the group alive, and if something goes wrong, others have a place to point the finger. But in this place I feel stronger in my faith and in myself than I ever have. I am still trying to decide if it is this place or the people I meet, though it is probably a combination of both. When I volunteered for this job, I didn't realize what I had gotten myself into; there are some difficult parts, but overall it is fulfilling.

Ours is a small group of soldiers; on a slow day we number around ten, but when we all show up, we are over twenty strong. We are a cross section of the militaries, Army, Air Force, and Marines; some of us do Intelligence work, some are network administrators, others mechanics. Still others go out on the streets and highways in an attempt to secure this nation. We are of various paths ranging from Greencraft to Asatru; in this place we form our eclectic Circle. We share with one another, we learn from one another, and we have fellowship, a place to relax and be ourselves: not just soldiers but Pagan soldiers. We blend our values with those the military gives us, living by honor, ethics, and our morals. By being here and being public in nature, we help dispel many of the misconceptions about our religion. We openly invite any and all visitors to our weekly circle and our rituals. I feel we are here to practice and to educate.

Our group was given a loss back in May when one of our members passed over; a roadside bomb claimed him. It forced all of us to look at our lives, our jobs, and what they mean in terms of our families and loved ones. All decided that this was what we do for a living, and that we would honor our fallen by continuing our mission in this life. His family is one of the many fighting for a pentacle on his headstone. We do not intend to let our brother down, and it is up to us to have our government honor his last request as he honored his oath to them.[15]

The author of this journal entry supported the passing of the law allowing the Wiccan pentacle to be engraved on tombstones. As mentioned earlier, this law was passed in April 2007.

In the following chapter, you'll gain a "sneak peek" into the lives of the fascinating and eclectic practitioners of Wicca. We'll share some exciting stories and list some of the most vital lessons we learned from those of pagan faiths.

Engaging the Seeker

Wicca and Its Practitioners

"People like to have new answers to old questions."
—Dr. Darrell Bock, author and
professor, Dallas Theological Seminary[1]

A teen girl makes a mad dash to stash her crystals and candles in her bedroom closet before her mother comes upstairs.

A business executive hides his Wiccan paraphernalia in his office desk drawer before his boss enters.

A group of Wiccan women meet in a stairwell to perform a ritual and share in fellowship during their lunch break from work.

Still in the Shadows

All over the world, Wiccans still feel they have to hide their faith and practices from a culture that just doesn't understand. So far, we've spent 12 chapters deepening our understanding of Wicca. But what about solving the riddle and gaining a greater understanding of Wiccans themselves? Can we unwrap this enigma to find out more about who these people of faith really are and what makes them tick? We need to, because that's the only way we'll be able to love and serve them effectively.

Of course, each person is unique, created specially in the image of God. And even discovering who might be a Wiccan in the first place can be a challenge. According to a recent newspaper article, at least half of Wiccans actively hide their faith from their relatives, and many also hide their faith from their employers.[2]

One such person is James (not his real name), a 58-year-old former Roman Catholic who has been an auditor for 30 years in what he calls "one of the most buttoned-down departments in one of the most sacrosanct agencies" of the federal government.

"I put on this Joe Taxpayer suit, and it's like living two lives," he said. "A minority would have a problem with me, but it would be a big problem. They would assume we are doing weird things, illegal, immoral things, at all hours. They wouldn't want to really know what we do, but they would go with their presuppositions instead."

James said that by "coming out of the broom closet," he risked ostracism at work and perhaps being pushed into early retirement, which would affect his pension. "I don't even want to contemplate it," he said.[3]

RELIGION *in the* CITY

A New York marketing executive finds his city so secular that being passionate about religion is often met with a smirk, and it would be worse if people knew he was Wiccan. "In my personal and private life, I like to be taken seriously," he said. "Pagans are associated with the '70s and hippies and counterculture. New York is a Type A city, and it's all about getting ahead, and the kooky ones don't get ahead."[4]

A Brief Look at Postmodernism

Christian author Madeleine L'Engle once wrote, "Jesus wasn't a theologian. He was God who told stories."[5] In some ways, this is true. Jesus didn't come to preach dry, boring theology; He came to tear the blinders off people's eyes and reveal to them that they could have abundant life if they would only place their faith fully in God.

Another author describes it this way:

> There's a Jewish saying: "God created man because he loves stories." I think that has a lot of truth to it. But not only

does God love stories, he loves the people whose stories are being told moment by moment across the globe. And I am amazed that the story of my choices, mistakes, regrets—the story of my life—actually matters to God.

I think what makes us unique isn't so much our height or shape or fingerprints or eye color but our histories, our stories. Day by day our lives are woven into a giant narrative, and every moment we become more and more the story of who we are. We *are* our stories. And we only connect with other people when we know their stories. The more intimate we are, the more our stories intertwine. That's one reason divorce is so painful—because it rips a single, deeply threaded story apart into two.

Sometimes I think about all the billions of stories swirling around each other on this planet, touching, deepening, unfurling, unraveling. And each one of those stories, each one of those people, mattered so much to the Author of Life that he left heaven and began the dreadful trek to the cross (see John 3:16). The original script called for unity and harmony, but our first parents [Adam and Eve] chose to derail the story of humanity into a graveyard.

"Okay," said the Creator. "Then I'll tell a new story. One that includes a detour through an empty tomb." But to make that tale come true, he had to enter our story himself.

When Jesus was born, the Word of God became flesh, enmeshed in a story. The storyteller entered the tale. The author stepped onto the page. The poet whose very words had written the cosmos became part of the text of this world.

Like the harmony and the melody living together in the same song, Jesus was divinity and humanity living together in the same heart. He was the Word of God, God's story, in the flesh.[6]

Jesus wasn't a stuffy Pharisee or a condemning preacher who

called down fire and brimstone on people. Instead, He captivated people's hearts and fired up their imaginations by revealing God's kingdom in story form. He showed people how their smaller stories fit into God's eternal plan for humanity.

Jesus breathed life into every story He told—which makes sense, because He was an author too. Hebrews 12:2 reminds us to "fix our eyes on Jesus, *the author and perfecter of our faith*, who for the joy set before him endured the cross, scorning its shame, and sat down at the right hand of the throne of God."

Jesus is the author of the unfolding narrative of our faith. We can entrust our life's creative stories to Him; He has already completed the work of salvation. He has had the last word![7]

Story's Place in Postmodernism

The generations categorized as GenY, Millennials, and Mosaics (those born between 1984 and 2002) primarily view life in story form. They've been taught to think differently. How? They've been exposed to fast-edit videos, computers, TV, iPods, iPhones, video games, and more, all of which now are being used in classrooms and homes all over the U.S.

All of these elements have taught young people, "You don't have to connect the dots the way your parents did. All you have to do is just react to whatever you see out there and—as long as it feels good, as long as you can make some sense out of it—that's good enough."[8]

In my interviews with Wiccans, I (Marla) discovered that their *experiences* have been key in influencing them to choose Wicca. Their experiences reflect a variety of tenets of postmodern philosophy, including the following:

+ "Relationships are vital; I need to be a part of a supportive community."

+ "Being authentic is crucial."

+ "We all create our own reality."

+ "There is no absolute truth, so for me to judge others would be wrong."

+ "We must protect the earth."

+ "I can't stand being controlled or told what to do."

+ "Experience and emotion are more important than knowledge and truth."

+ "Story and drama are paramount; everyone's story is a part of a larger narrative."

+ "It's important to be tolerant; you accept my views as good and I'll accept your views as good."

+ "Being a unique individual matters. Make your own decisions. Be yourself!"

+ "Guard yourself against consumerism. Strive to live a simpler life."

+ "We can rewrite history to say what we want it to say."

+ "There are no easy answers to life's most vital questions."[9]

Playing Down the Danger

Based on my research and personal interviews with witches, I sense that the relaxed rules, environmental emphasis, and positive attitude toward women are what attract most people to Wicca. One reporter stated, "Wicca appeals to a wide variety of people because of its clear feminist credentials and absence of homophobia."[10]

But another reason for Wicca's appeal is that our culture continues to play down Wicca's dangers. For example, Wiccan author Margot Adler implored,

> We are not evil. We don't harm or seduce people. We are not dangerous. We are ordinary people like you. We have families, jobs, hopes, and dreams. We are not a cult. This religion is not a joke. We are not what you think we are

from looking at T.V. We are real. We laugh, we cry. We are serious. We have a sense of humor. You don't have to be afraid of us. We don't want to convert you. And please don't try to convert us. Just give us the same right we give you—to live in peace. We are much more similar to you than you think.[11]

While I respect Adler's comments, I'm concerned by her plea, "Please don't try to convert us." Let's examine the reasons why, as Christians, we do feel compelled to reach out and share our beliefs with people of other faiths, including Wicca.

Reasons to Reach Out

First, we reach out and discuss matters of faith with people because we love them and we want them to know the truth. People have swallowed a lie, and we want them to taste the Living Water. It's exciting to help people discover the real truth about God and His plan for their lives.

Second, we desire to share the gospel with them because we're commanded to do so in Scripture. Jesus told His followers to "go into all the world and preach the good news to all creation" (Mark 16:15), so that's what we do.

Third, we feel compelled to create a dialogue about faith because we see people living in depression, sin, and despair. We want to help them snap off the shackles and break free from spiritual, emotional, and physical bondage so they can live the abundant life God has promised.

Clearly, most Wiccans believe we are "doing them a favor" by not ever engaging them in a theological conversation or sharing our faith with them. But is that really true?

The Bible states that "the message of the cross is foolishness to those who are perishing, but to us who are being saved it is the power of God" (1 Corinthians 1:18). To those who are drowning in sin, their way seems like the right way, but it only leads to death and destruction.

The following Bible verses provide strong warnings for those who refuse to seek the one true God and instead look to other gods or religious systems:

+ "Do not turn to mediums or seek out spiritists, for you will be defiled by them. I am the LORD your God" (Leviticus 19:31).

+ "How long, O men, will you turn my glory into shame? How long will you love delusions and seek false gods?" (Psalm 4:2).

+ "In his pride the wicked does not seek him; in all his thoughts there is no room for God" (Psalm 10:4).

+ "He who is not with me is against me, and he who does not gather with me scatters" (Matthew 12:30).

+ "He who has the Son has life; he who does not have the Son of God does not have life" (1 John 5:12).

These are some powerful passages, containing some serious warnings! But thankfully, God also makes some incredible promises to those who choose to seek Him. And He keeps His promises too. Check out some of them below:

+ "Seek first his kingdom and his righteousness, and all these things will be given to you as well" (Matthew 6:33).

+ "God did this so that men would seek him and perhaps reach out for him and find him, though he is not far from each one of us" (Acts 17:27).

+ "Without faith it is impossible to please God, because anyone who comes to him must believe that he exists and that he rewards those who earnestly seek him" (Hebrews 11:6).

The Bible contains a simple formula, actually: "Seek God and obey Him. Confess your sin and believe in His Son, and He will be faithful to forgive your sins, bless you, and grant you eternal life."

On the other hand, it also reveals what will happen to those who refuse to accept God's generous offer of abundant and eternal life with Him—and those who pretend to follow Him, but don't experience a true heart change. God will tell them plainly, "I never knew you. Away from me, you evildoers!" (Matthew 7:23).

How to Reach Out to a Wiccan

I asked Jessica (not her real name) what her past experiences had been with Christians. From the look on her face, I could tell they hadn't been positive. "They preach; they don't even listen," she said. "But you have to give respect to get respect. People are taught 'no tolerance.' They are afraid of what's different from them. A lot of people believe that Wiccans are all basically Satan-worshipping, gay child molesters."

I looked at her in surprise; this had not been my perspective of Wiccans at all.

"Hollywood is a lot to blame for the persecution of witches," she continued. "When you see a witch, she usually ends up to be the bad, black-magic type. And that first exposure sticks with you. It's mostly due to *Buffy the Vampire Slayer.* The character Willow came out as a lesbian. [She was a witch who later became a Wiccan.] When she 'came out of the broom closet,' it drew a lot of attention to witchcraft and caused people to get the wrong idea about what witches are like."

"So how can Christians do a better job of creating dialogue with Wiccans?" I asked.

"First of all, don't say, 'You're going to hell.' Try compassion and listen to the person's beliefs first to gain some sort of understanding. And do not call Wicca a cult to our faces!"

I appreciate Jessica's honest advice. It's a good reminder for me, and for all of us.

An Acronym for "Wiccan"

To summarize my experiences with Wiccans, I created an acronym for some of the most important lessons I learned while working on this book. My conversations with Wiccans revealed them to be talented, intelligent people with kind hearts and sensitive spirits. I learned so much from them, and I'm committed to becoming better friends with them and continuing the dialogue that we have established.

HOW *to* CONNECT

Kindness and genuine concern open doors; hasty judgment just slams them shut.

In the future, when you interact with those of pagan faiths, try to stifle your initial stereotypes and at least give people a chance to share their beliefs with you. You'll be amazed at how much you have in common with them—and how much you'll learn when you choose to listen first and talk later. Keep in mind the following acronym, and you'll be well on your way to establishing positive relationships with those of other faiths.

W*ise.* I found Wiccans to be wise people in a cultural sense, seasoned with life experience and able to share their beliefs in an effective way. Many younger pagans seemed wise beyond their years, partly due to the pain and persecution they have faced and the depth of their search for truth. They were dedicated to seeking greater knowledge and were committed to their faith.

I*ntuitive.* Wiccans are, above all, spiritual people. They feel at one with the earth, with nature, with animals, and with other humans. They trust their hearts and usually try to make decisions according to the effects that those decisions may have on other people. They consider the consequences of their actions. Most of them seek to do acts that will bring only good to others.

C*ompassionate.* The Wiccans I met surprised me with their sensitivity, compassion, and openness. Most of them seemed kindhearted and soft-spoken. I never had an argument with any of the people I interviewed. While we may not have agreed with each other's views, we were able to honor and appreciate our differences while sharing our beliefs. I genuinely liked the people I met.

Conscientious. I appreciated Wiccans' care and concern for the environment. They know how to practice what they preach! They follow through on their commitment to care for the earth and for other people. They practice their religion with a constant awareness of how their lives and their choices affect the lives of others.

Articulate. The Wiccans I met shared their views in an articulate manner. I appreciated their ability to provide insight on a wide variety of topics related to Wicca and environmental issues. Many of the young women, especially, astonished me with their insight and their ability to put their faith into words. They did an excellent job of explaining the tenets of Wicca and how people live them out.

No relationship. Though I grew to have immense respect for Wiccans, and even for many of the tenets of their faith, I had to remind myself of the bottom line: They do not have a relationship with the living God. They do not know Jesus Christ as their personal Savior. And that saddens me. It also motivates me to continue to model a vibrant faith to all those I meet.

In the following chapter, we'll discover how the principles and belief system of Wicca compare with those of Christianity. Dillon will offer you a simple, effective method for understanding how the systems are similar and also of the fundamental differences between them. Read on, as this chapter is crucial for equipping you to effectively share your faith with a Wiccan.

Knowing the Truth

Wicca and Christianity Compared

"All religions have one ideal at their core: to unite their followers with Deity. Wicca is no different."

—Scott Cunningham[1]

O ne of my biggest frustrations as I (Dillon) began to investigate Wicca's growing influence was the lack of discussion about the actual differences between Christianity and Wicca. Some books provided a quick gloss on the subject, while others painted Wicca as something it was not.

As we investigated the writings of leading Wiccan thinkers, we saw that this weakness also was true of their characterizations of biblical Christianity. Many suggested that Christianity was an inclusive religion, that the Bible offered support for the practices of witchcraft, or even that Jesus was some sort of misunderstood sorcerer or magical wizard.

Philip S. Johnson summarizes this issue well:

> The historical relationship between Craft and Church has not been a very good one. Wiccans have many justifiable reasons for being upset with and wary of Christians. There are two primary reasons. One is the way witches have been persecuted by the Church in Europe and North America. The other is that most Christian books about contemporary witchcraft badly misrepresent and distort it.[2]

The Essentials

As we compare Wicca with Christianity at a glance, we can see numerous contrasts between the two belief systems:[3]

Belief	What Wicca Says	What the Bible Says
Who God is (and isn't)	Wicca doesn't make a clear distinction between humanity and Deity. God consists of the Goddess (female) and the God (male). These two are equal, though the Goddess created the God.	There is one Triune God who consists of Father, Son, and Holy Spirit. God is Spirit (neither male nor female).
Who Jesus is	A spiritual leader, though opinions of Him vary greatly.	The Son of God and the second person of the Triune God.
What the Bible is	A spiritual book often used to promote discrimination against Wiccans.	Revelation from God Himself as expressed through human authors. Authoritative on all issues of faith.
View of humanity and our disconnection from God	There is no biblical concept of personal sin and no resulting need to be redeemed from anything.	All people have sinned (committed wrongs) and are separated from God.
How we connect with the Divine	There are many ways to connect with the Goddess and the God.	No one comes to God the Father except through Jesus (John 14:6; Acts 4:12).

| **What happens in the afterlife** | Most believe in reincarnation, with some believing in an ultimate afterlife in the Summerland. | There is only one life on earth followed by eternity with God in heaven (for believers) or apart from God in hell (for unbelievers). |

In addition to these essential beliefs, we find further aspects relating to Wicca in the pages of the Bible. We'll discuss them below.

HOW NOT to DISCUSS THEOLOGICAL DIFFERENCES WITH WICCANS

In an online article, Philip Johnson writes, "I recall participating in an Internet chat room sponsored by a Christian. The chat room was ostensibly open to all comers, and on one occasion, an Irish practitioner of Wicca dropped by. This person had no sooner identified herself as a practitioner when the regular Christian participants started shooting off quick one-liners about the devil, demons, hell and the like. There was no attempt by these Christians to become acquainted with her and treat her with respect. There was not the slightest effort made to discover what it is that she actually believed. Instead she was treated belligerently to the chat-room equivalent of a space-invaders game where she was the target of invective and abuse. I was sickened and apologized to her, whilst vainly trying to inject some sanity into the chat room at the same time." [4]

Biblical Passages Specific to Wicca and Witchcraft

Though Wiccans often argue that Christianity is compatible with Wicca, several biblical passages provide clear instructions for followers of Christ to avoid many Wiccan practices. These warnings can be organized into four major categories:

1. Warnings Against Worshipping Other Gods

The Bible explicitly states that only God must be worshipped and revered. The first of the Ten Commandments commands that God-followers must worship the Lord and serve Him only (Exodus 20:2-3; Deuteronomy 6:4-5). Not only is this an exhortation for us to worship one God, but it's also a command to worship the particular God described by Moses in the Torah—the God of Abraham, Isaac, and Jacob.

2. Warnings Against Worshipping Nature

The apostle Paul wrote to the followers of Christ in Rome about those who worshipped nature, stating, "They exchanged the truth of God for a lie, and worshiped and served created things rather than the Creator—who is forever praised. Amen" (Romans 1:25).

God created our universe, our planet, and everything in it (Genesis 1–2). As a result, how our environment is treated should be an important issue for Christians. However, to worship nature in any way is outside the boundaries of the Bible's teachings. Wiccans may say they do not worship creation, but they commonly hold the view that everything is God or part of God, meaning that animals and vegetables and trees are just as sacred as human life. (This is also a teaching of Buddhism and other Eastern religions.) While these beings and objects are sacred because they were created by God, they are still *distinct from God*.

Genesis tells us that God created the earth and entrusted its care to humans. He said: "Be fruitful and multiply. Fill the earth and govern it. Reign over the fish in the sea, the birds in the sky, and all the animals that scurry along the ground" (1:28 NLT; see also 2:15). The God of the Bible values all created life; however, He also places a clear priority on human life over other forms of creation.

A practical application of this principle is that both the elimination of starvation and the protection of the environment are critical Christian issues, yet Christian theology places a priority on preserving human life whenever a decision must be made between the two.

3. Warnings Against Practicing Witchcraft and Magic

Though magic and the casting of spells are considered positive (and not harmful) by those within Wicca, the Bible specifically condemns these practices. God warned Israel when they were about to enter the land He was giving them,

> Let no one be found among you who sacrifices his son or daughter in the fire, who practices divination or sorcery, interprets omens, *engages in witchcraft, or casts spells, or who is a medium or spiritist or who consults the dead.* Anyone who does these things is detestable to the LORD, and because of these detestable practices the LORD your God will drive out those nations before you. You must be blameless before the LORD your God.
>
> The nations you will dispossess listen to those who practice sorcery or divination. But as for you, the LORD your God has not permitted you to do so (Deuteronomy 18:10-14).

The New Testament also illustrates this principle. Paul had been commanding evil spirits to leave people in the city of Ephesus (in modern-day Turkey). Seven Jewish men copied his practice and, using the name of Jesus, tried to command an evil spirit to leave a man. The spirit rebelled and fought with the seven men until they ran away. The Bible then says,

> The story of what happened spread quickly all through Ephesus, to Jews and Greeks alike. A solemn fear descended on the city, and the name of the Lord Jesus was greatly honored. *Many who became believers confessed their sinful practices. A number of them who had been practicing sorcery brought their incantation books and burned them at a public bonfire.* The value of the books was several million dollars. So the message about the Lord spread widely and had a powerful effect (Acts 19:17-20 NLT).

Those who practiced the casting of spells and incantations were doing something that God considered wrong. When some of these people in Ephesus began to follow Christ, they burned their spell books as an outward sign of their changed lives. It was also an affirmation that they saw spell casting as something that dishonored God.

4. Warnings Against Communicating with Spirits and the Dead

Though many Wiccans do not participate in communicating with spirits or the spirits of the dead, some do. This particular practice is condemned in several biblical passages as unacceptable for those who follow and worship the God of the Bible (Deuteronomy 18:9-12; 2 Chronicles 33:2-6).[5]

The first witch mentioned in the Bible was in 1 Samuel 28. A witch lived in secrecy in Endor (not the same Endor as in *Return of the Jedi!*), and King Saul came to her in disguise at night for her help. He asked the medium (or "witch" in some translations) to bring up the spirit of the prophet Samuel. She attempted to complete his request, and then shrieked when the spirit of Samuel appeared (apparently this was different from her normal spirit encounters). Samuel condemned the actions of King Saul and predicted his death, the death of his sons, and the loss by his army the next day, all of which occurred as foretold.[6]

Saul had started his reign as the leader of Israel by enforcing the prohibition against witches and witchcraft. By the end of his life, he had turned to communicating with mediums and spirits in order to find help. This was a clear sign that he had turned from God's teachings, and he died shortly after this event occurred.

Again, not all Wiccans communicate with spirits, but those who do are participating in a practice that God's followers have been strictly instructed to avoid.

How to Share the Gospel with Pagans—According to a Pagan

Wiccan practitioner Gwydion Oak calls himself a former Christian turned Wiccan. His popular article "How to Share the Gospel with Pagans" has been viewed over 72,000 times online and has been cited in national media. His words of wisdom offer a rare perspective into the thoughts of a practicing Wiccan. His guidelines include, first, to *not attack Wiccans:*

> I make a point of reading every Christian tract on Paganism I encounter on the Internet or elsewhere, and the overwhelming majority of them are based on attacking Pagan religions and those who practice them as "evil," "devil-worshippers," and "calling them to repentance before they are doomed to hell forever." I have written to the authors of these tracts, asking exactly what they meant to accomplish by writing what they did. The two purposes that are always mentioned are…
>
> 1. to protect Christians from being "lured away" from the true faith.
>
> 2. to persuade Pagans to return to Christ.
>
> Unfortunately, attacks such as these usually fail totally on both counts.[7]

Oak's second recommendation is to *get your facts straight.* Again, the misrepresentation of Wicca by Christians and other non-Wiccans sets up a scenario in which we attempt to persuade Wiccans to turn away from something they don't believe in the first place. In his words, "Tract writers seem fascinated with the idea of animal and human sacrifice, and this is always included in lurid descriptions of alleged Pagan rituals. Do modern Pagans sacrifice animals or people? No. Did they do so in the ancient past? Possibly. Sacrifices were part of nearly all ancient religions, the Biblical Hebrews being no exception."

Gwydion also points out that Christians should *be honest about the "dark side" of Christianity* as well. Instead of arguing how many witches died at Salem, why not confess that it was a horrible tragedy that anyone was put to death for a different set of beliefs? Then focus on the positive aspects of the Christian faith.

Further, Gwydion shares that Christians must treat *pagans as people first*. He openly exposes the harmful attitudes of many well-meaning Christians in his own experience:

> Sometimes I was invited to their homes for dinner, sometimes to church social activities or services. There was a conspicuous effort to "get close" to me, and the topic of religion came up very often. This continued until it became clear that I wasn't going to jump into the baptismal pool right away, and that I was firmly committed to my religion. Then the "friendship" cooled off rapidly, phone calls ceased, and many times I was later treated with open hostility by the very people who had taken it upon themselves to approach me.[8]

Treating pagans as people first is good advice. What if we genuinely loved the unchurched (of all backgrounds) even if they never chose to follow Jesus?

Finally, Gwydion challenges Christians to accept that they will not reach every Wiccan. It doesn't mean we can't try. But if someone continues to say no, we are still challenged to treat the person with respect. As in many areas of life, we never know what God might do long term with that spiritual seed we have planted.

EVENTUAL FRUIT

We may be just the first seed sower in a pagan person's life. We don't know when God might bring along other faithful Christians to water and cultivate the seed, and the gospel message may eventually come to fruition in that person's life.

How Would You Respond?

One teenage Wiccan I (Dillon) spoke with—I'll call her Amber—is preparing to attend a well-known university in the Northeast as a drama major. She loves acting and hopes to become involved in some of the numerous theater productions in her new area.

A few people know of her involvement in the craft, but not many of her family members do. She doesn't think they would understand. But she says she feels peaceful. Connected. Happy.

But what happens when *you* run into your version of Amber in your community? How would you respond? Would you offer to help her get to know the community, or would you walk down a different aisle if you saw her in a store? Would you show her compassion, or would you be just another person who claims to follow Jesus but ignores or mistreats her?

Your version of Amber is out there. How are you going to approach her?

In our final chapter, Marla and I will each take a personal look at how investigating Wicca has actually helped to strengthen our faith as followers of Jesus. We'll also discuss a few other paradoxes we discovered along the way. We'll include some thoughts on how we hope to reach the Wiccans in our lives. And we hope you'll be surprised and challenged by some of our discoveries.

How Investigating Wicca
Strengthened Our Faith

(And Other Paradoxes Along the Way)

"Christians should be able to see that Wiccan views do indeed compel us to go back to Scripture for a deeper look and in doing that we might rediscover some biblical truths we have overlooked."

—Philip S. Johnson[1]

Both of us entered into our investigation of Wicca with certain ideas and stereotypes we thought would be true but were not. For example, we thought that all witches cast both good and evil spells. We later found out that some witches do *not* cast evil spells, as they believe that the negative consequences of performing dark magick will return to them threefold.

As we wrap up our journey together, we want to share some of our overall observations with you, our readers. In some ways, Wicca caused us to grow even deeper in our Christian faith. We encountered issues that caused us to want to reach out more to people and do an even better job of applying our Christian beliefs and convictions to our everyday lives. We think you'll be both surprised and inspired by our personal reflections on this *Generation Hex* journey.

Q: How did this journey strengthen your faith?

Marla: Writing this book empowered me to reflect more deeply and honestly on my faith and more closely examine the foundational truths of Scripture. It led me to study God and the person of Jesus in greater depth than I ever have before in order to find out why I believe God is who He says He is and Jesus truly is the Son of God. I was reminded afresh of how extraordinary the story of redemption is, and of all the ways Jesus differs from the leaders of other religions.

My interactions with Wiccans also reminded me that all people, everywhere, are spiritual beings. God created us that way. We desire a relationship with God, and we desire many other attributes as well: love, joy, truth, beauty, peace, fulfillment, freedom, safety, power, and purpose. If we, as Christians, don't demonstrate to people that the one true God provides all of these things, then they will turn to other sources and other gods.

Dillon: Investigating Wicca forced me to reevaluate what I believe. I once again found myself remembering how Christ has changed my broken life, revealed Himself to me through the Bible, and helped me live a life of purpose and meaning as I serve Him. As I thought back to how God has transformed me, it has rekindled my desire to communicate my story with anyone who will listen, whether their background is Wicca, Muslim, Hindu, or no faith at all.

The other way investigating Wicca has reshaped my faith is by giving me a deeper appreciation of other people. It's tough to talk about spirituality with someone for an extended period of time and not start to care about the other person. During my times of prayer and reflection, God continues to bring to mind many of the people I interviewed for this project. My genuine hope is to display Christ's love to some of them in such a compelling and authentic manner that they will at least say, "There is someone who is a Christian who really cares about me as a person."

Q: What surprised you in your investigation of Wicca?

Dillon: I really had to start over when I began to investigate Wicca. I'm a Christian trained in conservative evangelical theology, and most writing I had encountered about witchcraft was black-and-white, with no real attempt to create a dialogue with the people involved. And while there *are* some black-and-white issues that mark each system as a distinct faith, human lives that are involved are often trampled on.

For example, when a Wiccan discovered I was writing a book on Wicca from a Christian perspective, occasionally his or her communication would turn hostile. Every other Christian these people had encountered had shown them a life they wanted no part of.

Another surprise was that a lot of material written by Christians on Wicca is simply inaccurate. Witchcraft has been equated with Satanism, sexual promiscuity, and child abuse. I've found these assertions to be unfounded (at least in mainstream Wicca). Wiccans do not believe in Satan, are often loyal to one sexual partner, help the poor, care about the environment, and hold the highest concern for children. The truth is, Wiccans are often more friendly than the Christians who write about them.

Marla: I was surprised to discover that Wiccans were fantastic people to talk to. They were knowledgeable and kind. Most shared their experiences openly and did an excellent job of answering my questions.

I also learned that the quest for absolute truth is a thing of the past. Most postmoderns don't believe such a thing even exists. Instead, young people are searching for a true spiritual experience—they want what *works*. If they believe Wicca works, they'll follow it. If they believe Wicca offers them a desirable experience that Christianity doesn't, then they'll choose Wicca. If they believe magick actually gets results, then they'll keep practicing it.

I also was surprised to see how strongly young people today desire to return to a simpler life—a more ecologically aware, peaceful, nature-centered existence. Today's young people desperately want beauty and spirituality in their lives. People don't want to be preached at. They want to make their own choices, to feel as though they have some degree of power over their own existence. It's our responsibility to demonstrate the irresistibility of the gospel, the power and freedom it offers to all who believe in the one true God.

Q: What were the most important things you learned?

Marla: I learned that most of my preconceived ideas about Wicca and Wiccans were false. I quickly discovered the importance of listening first and talking later. I also learned to be careful in my interactions with Wiccans, as many of them have had difficult, heartbreaking experiences with Christianity or with Christians (though many of those Christians may have meant well).

Negative church experiences have caused millions of people to turn to Wicca and alternative religions and to turn *away* from Christianity. That's sad. We must first demonstrate Christ's love and earn the right to be heard before we start preaching to people about life change.

I love a quote by Catherine Edwards Sanders, author of *Wicca's Charm*. She said, "It's really very simple: Young people are seeking authentic spirituality. We have to respect their model of belief, strange as it may seem to us, before we can expect them to consider ours."[2]

Jesus loved people as they were, in their brokenness and their frailty. He often met their physical needs before He addressed their spiritual needs. He used conversations about their external condition to segue into addressing the condition of their souls. I think we can follow the same model as we reach out to people involved in Wicca and pagan spirituality.

Dillon: When I began to talk with those involved in various Wiccan groups, I noticed several things. First, Wicca is a faith system *and* a culture. It includes a unique set of beliefs, but also consists of a variety of specific habits, including celebrating holidays, using symbols, sharing values, and utilizing certain language.

One paradox I discovered is that those involved in Wicca are often *more relational* than many Christians. In my research I observed two primary types of people involved in Wicca. The first and largest group consisted of nature-loving individuals with a desire to connect spiritually with the people and world around them. I genuinely enjoyed my interactions with them and found many commonalities in areas of concern regarding the environment, family, human rights, and other issues.

The second group I discovered among Wiccans were those who had chosen Wicca in *reaction* to another form of religion—usually legalistic or fundamentalist Christianity. As soon as this minority group of Wiccans would discover my faith, they would become very closed off and negative toward me. While I understood the reason for their reaction, it was also frustrating. Some Wiccans have absorbed the discrimination given to them and now return it toward others like me who desire to build positive relationships and develop compassionate dialogue.

Q: What message do you think the church needs to hear?

Dillon: The most important revelation for me is that Wiccans are spiritually seeking people, just like me. Would Jesus have invested time in those involved in Wicca if they had lived in Israel during His time on earth? I'm sure He would have. They would have been very interested in His concerns for all creation, the poor, human rights, respect and value for women, and His love for all humanity.

If Jesus would have been interested in their lives, why shouldn't *I* be? If I consider myself to be a Christian (a word meaning "Christlike"), then why shouldn't I build relationships and show unconditional love to those who devote their lives to Wicca?

DILLON'S DECISION

My personal application from *Generation Hex* is to continue to build caring relationships with those involved in the craft so I can help point them toward Jesus, the only One who can fully satisfy their spiritual cravings in this life and for eternity.

The application for readers of this book and the church is the same: Jesus loves Wiccans, and so should we. Jesus was the one who said, "If you love only those who love you, why should you get credit for that? Even sinners love those who love them! And if you do good only to those who do good to you, why should you get credit? Even sinners do that much!" (Luke 6:32-33 NLT).

If we start by loving those involved in the craft, regardless of whether they become Christians or begin to attend our church, then we demonstrate what Jesus said: "Your love for one another will prove to the world that you are my disciples" (John 13:35 NLT).

I realize that many, especially those inside the church, may disagree with this conclusion. Yet rising to this challenge does not compromise my faith; the challenge is to live out my beliefs *among* those of differing faiths. Here's how the apostle Paul put it, again in *The Message* paraphrase:

> Even though I am free of the demands and expectations of everyone, I have voluntarily become a servant to any and all in order to reach a wide range of people: religious, nonreligious, meticulous moralists, loose-living immoralists, the defeated, the demoralized—whoever. I didn't take on their way of life. I kept my bearings in Christ—but I entered their world and tried to experience things from their point of view. *I've become just about every sort of servant there is in my attempts to lead those I meet into a God-saved life. I did all this because of the Message.* I didn't just want to talk about it; I wanted to be in on it! (1 Corinthians 9:19-23 MSG).

Those who follow the practices of Wicca collectively form a culture we are sent to reach out to with a mind-set of love, hospitality, and persuasive dialogue regarding who Jesus is. Jesus is not simply a good man or a great teacher. He's not a mythological figure. He is the Messiah who came from heaven to earth to provide a redemptive connection between the eternal Creator God and humanity.

Marla: In Romans 2:4, we learn that it's God's *kindness* that leads people to repentance. The Bible also says, "[The Lord] is patient with you, not wanting anyone to perish, but everyone to come to repentance" (2 Peter 3:9). He wants *every person* to come to the knowledge of Him.

We've been charged with an enormous responsibility: to reach out to those involved in Wicca and alternative religions. Sometimes it may be difficult, but the reward is so great. Paul taught in 1 Corinthians 1:18, "The message of the cross is foolishness to those who are perishing, but to us who are being saved it is the power of God." If we fail to reach out to those who are perishing, we are sinning against God and our fellow human beings. But being salt and light to the world is not just a commandment; it's a joy and a privilege.

Thank you for joining us on the journey.

Frequently Asked Questions (FAQs) About Wicca and Witchcraft

Not every question about Wicca and witchcraft could be answered in the chapters of this book. In this section, as a quick reference, we've included a few short responses to some of the most common questions we have received along the way.

Is Wicca a form of Satanism?

The short answer is no. Wiccans don't even believe in Satan's existence, so they don't worship him.

Some Christians argue that worshipping any other god besides God Almighty is worshipping Satan. This may be true in a roundabout way, but it's usually best to approach a Wiccan with the understanding that he or she is not consciously worshipping Satan. Wiccans believe in doing good deeds and in treating people, animals, and the earth with respect. Having this in mind will help you build more positive relationships with Wiccans and help you create a foundation for sharing the gospel with them.

Is the Wiccan pentacle a satanic symbol?

The pentacle (with the point up) and the pentagram (with the point down) are not "evil" symbols. The pentacle is never used as a satanic symbol; however, the pentagram is sometimes used that way. The two symbols are used differently by various religious movements. If you see someone wearing a pentacle or pentagram, don't immediately assume that the person is a Satan-worshipper. Rather than make accusations, use the opportunity to ask that person about his or her beliefs.

Do Wiccans sacrifice animals?

Wiccans do not typically sacrifice animals. Wiccans love animals and care intensely about protecting nature, including all types of wildlife. There are a few fringe groups who do practice animal sacrifices, but this is not the norm. Most animal sacrifices are performed by those involved in Satanism, not by Wiccans or those involved in New Age religions.

Do Wiccans cast evil spells on people?

Wiccans follow the Rule of Three, which says that a person's deeds (both good and bad) return to that person threefold. As a result, magick of any kind is not supposed to be used for harm or for evil purposes. However, people's definitions of what constitutes "harm" and "evil" may vary widely. Several of the Wiccans we interviewed admitted to casting both good and bad spells on people, but they regretted casting bad spells and thought they had experienced negative consequences as a result.

Are Wiccans involved in ritual orgies?

This practice is not condoned among modern Wiccans. This stereotype harks back to Wiccan writings from the 1960s that promoted witchcraft along with the practice of free sex and lots of other dicey stuff. As with many religious movements, however, there are exceptions.

Does Wicca promote homosexuality?

There is a vast difference between promoting homosexuality and accepting it. Wiccans generally find no problem with people practicing homosexuality, and they accept gay and lesbian members into their covens and communities. However, modern Wicca does not focus on homosexuality, as it considers a person's sexual preference to be just one aspect of life among many. You will more likely see a Wiccan talking about the environment with a passion than trying to promote his or her views on sexuality.

Do all witches wear black?

Only on television! Today's witches come in every style, ranging from business executives to military personnel to teenagers sporting the latest Abercrombie fashions. Your barista at the local coffee shop and the mayor of your city may very well be witches. Don't assume that a person who "looks like a witch" is one, and don't assume that other people aren't witches just because they don't fit the Goth stereotype.

Do Wiccans celebrate Christmas, Easter, or other traditional Christian holidays?

This varies. Some Wiccans on websites such as Witchvox.com have posted articles adamantly against the celebration of any Christian holiday. However, our research indicates that the majority of Wiccans celebrate the secular side of Christian holidays just as most Americans do. Most Wiccan holidays coincide closely with the dates of Christian holidays, so the celebrations may coincide as well.

Can Christians be involved in witchcraft, occult activities, or pagan ceremonies?

Biblically, the answer is a clear no. If you are in doubt, read Deuteronomy 18. According to the Torah (the first five books of the Old Testament), anyone involved in witchcraft was put to death. After the time of Jesus, Christians realized that non-Jews were not required to follow the laws of Moses (Acts 15), but there are also places in the New Testament that call involvement in witchcraft a sin. Galatians 5:19-21 lists witchcraft along with several other sins (envy, hatred, and alcoholism to name a few), teaching that those who live in these lifestyles will not inherit the kingdom of God.

In our research, we sometimes acted as observers of pagan ceremonies or watched footage of their activities, the way a journalist may visit a mosque or a church to report on the activity there. We did not participate in any pagan activities, but we wanted to be able to observe Wiccans' actions, interview them, and talk openly with them so we could represent their beliefs and practices as fairly and accurately as possible.

Are all witches female?

According to the most recent books and articles by Wiccan writers, about two-thirds of Wiccans are female. Wicca appeals strongly to women, partly because Wiccans believe the Deity consists of the Goddess and the God, and therefore is both male and female. However, many men are involved in witchcraft and Wicca, including some clergy, most of whom also call themselves witches. Other men involved in pagan faiths may call themselves wizards, warlocks, or sorcerers, but this is not as common.

Why is there so much animosity between Wiccans and Christians?

Wiccans might ascribe this tension to what they call the Burning Times, which is the period of medieval history in which the church officially condoned the murder of witches. Wiccans also believe that in more recent times, the Salem witch trials reveal Christians as the murderers of witches (or of people who were wrongly accused of witchcraft). This is certainly adequate reason for Wiccans to have a negative attitude toward the church and Christians.

Today, negative attitudes and stereotypes about Wicca and witchcraft remain, reinforcing discrimination. When Christians call people names or avoid contact with them because of their religious beliefs, what are pagan people supposed to think? They certainly don't feel loved or welcomed by Christians. The only way we can change this pattern is by showing genuine care toward those of different faiths, including Wiccans.

How can I talk about Jesus with someone involved in witchcraft?

First, you have to stop looking at Wiccans or those involved in witchcraft as what I (Dillon) call a "potential buyer of Christianity." People will know if you are showing interest in them only to convert them. When we think someone is talking to us just to sell us something, we automatically withdraw from that person. We don't think that he or she truly cares about us as an individual; we think he or she is just trying to sell us a product. The same is true in talking about Jesus with Wiccans.

We don't know exactly how to reach Wiccans and help them get to the point of making the decision to turn their lives over to Jesus, but we can tell you how to show them the love of Jesus. Treat them well. Listen to them. Smile. Be friendly. Care. When you do, people want to become more like you. They want the same joy that you have. When we see someone who radiates joy and shows real love, we automatically think, *I wish I could be more like her.* That's your goal. Once a person desires what you have, tell them, "It's Jesus. He's the difference-maker." Make your life and your actions stand out, and then you'll have the opportunity to tell people why you are so extraordinary. A life transformed by God speaks volumes!

Acknowledgments

Thank you for purchasing and reading *Generation Hex*. It is our hope that this book has encouraged you and provided you with some creative ways of connecting with those who are involved in Wicca and other alternative religions and communicating Christ's perfect love to them.

We especially want to thank our friends at Harvest House Publishers who have supported us throughout the development of this project, including Bob Hawkins Jr., Terry Glaspey, LaRae Weikert, Kimberly Shumate, Steve Miller, and Rod Morris. We couldn't have done it without you.

Most of all, we thank Jesus Christ, our Teacher, Leader, and Forgiver. All the glory goes to Him.

Dillon's Thanks...

My wife, Deborah, and children, Ben and Natalie; my friends at ATRI—John and Darlene Ankerberg, Alan Weathers, Michelle Ankerberg, Steve Humble, Jack Borders, Beth Lambertson, Marlene Alley, Ben Bronsink, Debbie Hayes, Beth Newsome, Jim Virkler, Ruth Wilson, and Esther Wilson; my friends at Woodland Park, especially Kelly O'Rear and Chris Gaither; my friends at TN Temple, especially Danny and Susan Lovett, David Kemp, Eddie Rhodes, Geoff Whitaker, Greg Stephens, and all of the students in my youth ministry courses (especially Josiah Goff, Tony Helton, and Josh Coffman); my prayer supporters, especially Dorothy Martin; my family—including my mom, Ron, Tiffany, Luis, Elizabeth, Travis, Sarah, Lily, and Claire; Roger and Rose Bear and everyone at BCM at Indiana State; my friends at White River—Tim Brock, Phil Heller, Keith Comp, Tammy Kalstead, Brian Hansen, and the rest of the staff; all my friends from back in the day at Campus Crusade; my profs and friends at Dallas Theological Seminary for training me in the truth and showing me how to live it out; my youth ministry students throughout the years at Northcrest, Fellowship Bible Dallas, and Sherman Bible—especially Gary Roe, Evan Myers, Jarod Olds, Mike and Jeni Squiers, and Ben Scholl—and my friends from FBC North Terre Haute—especially Mark Tobey, Pat Anders, and my good friend Tony Brown, who keeps serving God where he's planted.

Also, a special thanks to the numerous individuals and organizations who helped me better understand the thinking and practices of those involved in Wicca and witchcraft—Megan, Onyx Serpentfire at Coffee & A Spell in New York, Ariawn, Michael Lane, Peg and Fritz at Witchvox, Patti Wigington, and those who wished to remain unnamed in this book. I consider you friends and continue to mention you in my prayers.

And finally, a special thanks to my friends at Starbucks on Shallowford and Napier in Chattanooga, Tennessee, for some great early morning coffee while I was working on this project.

Marla's Thanks...

My deepest thanks and appreciation go out to my husband, Catalin, and my parents, Terry and Dorothy Martin, for their love and their fervent prayers for this project. A big thank you also goes out to my sisters and brothers: Dillon, Deborah, Benjamin, and Natalie; Doug; Colleen and Daryl; and Cecilia. Your light shines so brightly! Your laughter and encouragement make life worth living. Thanks too, to Dad, Joanna, Nadine, Eric, Dana, and Joey. May God continue to bless each of you!

Thank you to our amazing support team at First Baptist Church in North Terre Haute. Your prayers mean the world to us. Special thanks to Mark and Tracy Tobey, Pat and Becky Anders, and all the other friends and family members from FBCNTH who encouraged us and prayed for us. You proved that the prayers of a righteous person are powerful and effective.

Thank you to our incredible friends at Stonebriar Community Church in Frisco, Texas. We deeply appreciate your friendship and your prayers. Also, a big thank you to my pals in the Frisco Writers Group, including Pat Verbal and Chonda Ralston. And thank you to my Mount Hermon friends and the Yahoo Writers' Group. I appreciate your encouragement.

Also, a heartfelt thank you to my friends, writing teachers, mentors, and fellow authors, including Abbi Wright, Tammy and Steve Labuda, Valerie and Rusty Reynolds, Crystal and Bobby Bosse, Liliam and Jason Gardner, Sarah and David Morgan, Elena and Gil Acevedo, Amy and Kywin Supernaw, Amy Joy and Layne Olivo, Jen and Joe Stolz, Nicole Carryl, Heidi and Lamar Jostes, Suzanne Keffer, Jen and Brian Goins, Stephanie and Mike Svigel, Marianne Boruch, Mary and Patrick DeMuth, Carol and James Frugé, Sandra and Gary Glahn, Ava and Greg Smith, Amy and Wes Zell, and Lauren and Kevin Scott. It's good to be walking this path with you. You're a blessing, and your prayers for us and for this book have been deeply felt.

Thanks to my professors at Purdue University, Liberty Seminary, and Dallas Theological Seminary for your excellent teaching and constant support. You taught me to "be Jesus with skin on" to all those around me. Special thanks to Sandi Glahn and Oscar Lopez. Your words of kindness and encouragement will never be forgotten.

Now to him who is able to do immeasurably more than all we ask or imagine, according to his power that is at work within us, to him be glory in the church and in Christ Jesus throughout all generations, for ever and ever! Amen.

—Ephesians 3:20-21

Chapter 1—Wicca 101

1. Phyllis Curott, "Everything You Ever Wanted to Know about Wicca..." www.phylliscurott .com/facts.doc.

2. From a personal interview by Dillon Burroughs. Used with permission. Name has been changed.

3. Catherine Edwards, "Wicca Casts Spell on Teen-Age Girls," as quoted in *Insight* online, vol. 15, no. 39, October 25, 1999.

4. According to the American Religious Identification Survey (2001), the top religious groups were 1) Christianity (159,030,000); 2) Nonreligious/Secular (27,539,000); and 3) Judaism (2,831,000). Wiccans were listed at only 307,000 at the time, though many Wiccans and Pagans do not identify Wicca as their official religion, and some practice multiple religions. See http://adherents.com/rel_USA.html for a complete list.

5. Cited by Steve Wohlberg in *Hour of the Witch* (Shippensburg, PA: Destiny Image, 2005), 15.

6. Wohlberg, 18.

7. Quoted by Kimberly Winston in "The Witch Next Door," *BeliefNet.com*. Accessed at www .beliefnet.com/story/155/story_15517.html.

8. Religious Tolerance.org, www.religioustolerance.org/wic_faq.htm. Accessed on July 3, 2007.

9. According to the organization's own information. Accessed at www.wicca.org/church/ Milestones.html.

10. Cited by Catherine Edwards Sanders in *Wicca's Charm* (Colorado Springs: Shaw Books, 2005), 25.

11. See www.witchvox.com/vn/vn_detail/dt_gr.html?a=usnc&id=22029.

12. See www.llewellyn.com.

13. Todd Leopold, "Midnight About to Toll for 'Harry Potter'," CNN.com, July 20, 2007. Accessed at www.cnn.com/2007/SHOWBIZ/books/07/19/potter.advancer/index .html#cnnSTCText.

14. As of July 24, 2007.

15. Adapted from Winston.

16. "New Research Explores Teenage Views and Behavior Regarding the Supernatural," *Barna Update*, January 23, 2006. Accessed at www.barna.org/FlexPage.aspx?Page=BarnaUpdate &BarnaUpdateID=216.

17. "New Research."

18. "Harry Potter's Influence Goes Unchallenged in Most Homes and Churches," *Barna Update*, May 1, 2006. Accessed at www.barna.org/FlexPage.aspx?Page=BarnaUpdate& BarnaUpdateID=237.

Chapter 2—The Harry Potter Factor

1. Raymond Buckland, *Wicca for One: The Path of Solitary Witchcraft* (New York: Citadel Press, 2004), vii.

2. This article, "What Every Person Should Know about Harry Potter 7," may still be downloaded for free at www.johnankerberg.org.

3. See the full list of awards and nominations at www.imdb.com/title/tt0241527/.

4. See www.potterwatch.com/mpn/html/article.php?sid=302&mode=thread&order=0&t hold=0.

5. See www.mpaa.org/FlmRat_Ratings.asp.

6. J.K. Rowling, notes from an interview at the Edinburgh Book Festival, August 15, 2004. Accessed at www.jkrowling.com/textonly/en/news_view.cfm?id=80.

7. See www.hp-lexicon.org/magic/occlumency.html.

8. Michael O'Brien, *A Landscape with Dragons* (San Francisco: Ignatius Press, 1998), 110–111.

9. Two organizations with helpful resources in this area include johnankerberg.org and plug gedinonline.com.

10. "Harry Potter's Influence Goes Unchallenged in Most Homes and Churches," Barna Update, May 1, 2006. Accessed at www.barna.org/FlexPage.aspx?Page=BarnaUpdate& BarnaUpdateID=237.

Chapter 3—The (New) Old Ways

1. From a personal interview by Marla Alupoaicei. Used with permission. Name has been changed.

2. Marion L. Starkey, *The Devil in Massachusetts: A Modern Enquiry into the Salem Witch Trials* (New York: Anchor Books, 1989), 175.

3. Scott Cunningham, *Wicca: A Guide for the Solitary Practitioner* (St. Paul, MN: Llewellyn Publications, 2001), xiv.

4. Laurie Cabot, as quoted by Catherine Edwards Sanders in *Wicca's Charm* (Colorado Springs: Shaw Books, 2005), 13.

5. Denise Zimmermann and Katherine A. Gleason, revised with Miria Liguana, *The Complete Idiot's Guide to Wicca and Witchcraft*, 3rd ed. (New York: Alpha Books, 2006), 9.

6. Sanders, 4.

7. Phyllis Curott, as quoted by Sanders, 9.

8. Silver RavenWolf, *Llewellyn's 1999 Magickal Almanac* (St. Paul, MN: Llewellyn Publishers, 1998), as cited at www.religioustolerance.org/wic_hist.htm.

9. Tim Baker, *Dewitched* (Nashville: Transit Books, Thomas Nelson, 2004), 28-29.

10. Steve Russo, *What's the Deal with Wicca?* (Minneapolis: Bethany House Publishers, 2005), 27.

11. Herne, "What is Wicca?" www.wicca.com/celtic/wicca/wicca.htm.

12. "Development," A Brief History of Wicca, copyright © 1997–2006, Church and School of Wicca. See www.wicca.org/church/WiccaOutline.html.

13. "Wicca's World: Looking into the Pagan Phenomenon," a *Zenit Daily Dispatch*, Amsterdam, Netherlands, 26 November, 2005. See www.ewtn.com/library/ISSUES/zwicca.HTM.

14. Drawn from the transcript of a presentation given by Julia Phillips at a Wiccan conference in Canberra, Australia, in 1991. The full article appears at www.tradwicca.org/englandhistory.html.

15. Phillips.

16. 1999 *World Book Encyclopedia*, see "Witch."

17. Anne Niven, as quoted by Sanders, 5.

18. Scott Cunningham, *The Truth About Witchcraft Today* (St. Paul, MN: Llewellyn Publications, 1987), 2.

19. From a personal interview by Marla Alupoaicei. Used with permission.

20. Luna Morgan, "O Say Can You See," The Witches' Voice, www.witchvox.com. Posted on 11 November 2007.

21. Donald Miller, *Blue Like Jazz* (Nashville: Thomas Nelson, 2003), 192.

22. Baker, 37.

Chapter 4—The Book of Shadows

1. Richard G. Howe, "Modern Witchcraft: It May Not Be What You Think," *Christian Research Journal*, vol. 28, no. 1 (2005). Accessed at www.equip.org/atf/cf/percent7B9C4EE03A-F988-4091-84BD-F8E70A3B0215 percent7D/JAW188.pdf.

2. Gary Cantrell, *Wiccan Beliefs and Practices* (St. Paul, MN: Llewellyn Publications, 2006), 45.

3. Cantrell, 48.

4. The Council of American Witches disbanded soon afterward. This organization no longer exists.

5. Denise Zimmermann and Katherine A. Gleason, revised with Miria Liguana, *The Complete Idiot's Guide to Wicca and Witchcraft*, 3rd ed. (New York: Alpha Books, 2006), 60-61.

6. This section is adapted from Dillon's chapter on Wicca in John Ankerberg and Dillon Burroughs, *What's the Big Deal About Other Religions?* (Eugene, OR: Harvest House Publishers, 2008).

7. From www.magicwicca.com/wicca/definition.html.

8. Dillon Burroughs, Keith Brooks, and Irvine Robertson, *Comparing Christianity with the Cults* (Chicago: Moody Publishing, 2007).

9. Raven Grimassi, *The Wiccan Mysteries: Ancient Origins and Teachings* (St. Paul, MN: Llewellyn Publications, 2000), 100.

10. From "The Summerland" at http://en.wikipedia.org/wiki/The_Summerland.

11. Scott Cunningham, *Wicca: A Guide for the Solitary Practitioner* (St. Paul, MN: Llewellyn Publications, 2006), xiii.

Chapter 5—The Wide, Wide World of Wicca

1. Eileen Holland, *The Wiccan Handbook* (Boston: Weiser Books, 2000), 16.

2. Steve Russo, *What's the Deal with Wicca?* (Minneapolis: Bethany House Publishers, 2005), 46.

3. Gary Cantrell, *Wiccan Beliefs and Practices* (St. Paul, MN: Llewellyn Publications, 2006), 49.

4. From "FAQs about Wicca," at www.faqs.org/faqs/religions/wicca/faq/.

5. Scott Cunningham, *Living Wicca* (St. Paul, MN: Llewellyn Publications, 2005), 10.

6. Cunningham, 59.

7. Cunningham, 61.

8. Cunningham, 61.

9. Cunningham, 4.

10. From "Wicca" at http://en.wikipedia.org/wiki/Wicca.

11. Cunningham, 15.

12. Quotations found at Pagan Spirit Gathering website at www.circlesanctuary.org/psg/ memories.

13. From "Celtic/Neopagan Handfasting," ReligiousTolerance.org. Accessed at http:// en.wikipedia.org/wiki/Handfasting.

14. Cunningham, 63-70.

15. Ann-Marie Gallagher, *The Wicca Bible* (New York: Sterling Publishing Co., Inc., 2005), 27.

16. From "Wicca" at http://en.wikipedia.org/wiki/Wicca.

17. Daniel Pye, "Cup & A Spell: Coffee Shop Offers Gourmet Drinks and Fortune Telling," *The Tonawanda News*, 7 September 2007. Accessed at www.tonawanda-news.com/ business/gnnbusiness_story_250124707.html?keyword=topstory. Also see www.coffee andaspell.com/index.html.

18. This coffee shop has since closed and has reopened as a different business.

19. Dan Kimball, *They Like Jesus, but Not the Church* (Grand Rapids, MI: Zondervan, 2006), 185.

Chapter 6—In Gods and Goddesses We Trust

1. Scott Cunningham, *Wicca: A Guide for the Solitary Practitioner* (St. Paul, MN: Llewellyn Publications, 2006), 5.

2. Jennifer, as posted on Facebook. Used with permission. Name has been changed.

3. "Explicit Religious Doctrines," *A Brief History of Wicca,* copyright © 1997–2006, Church and School of Wicca. See www.wicca.org/church/WiccaOutline.html.

4. Cunningham, 11-12.

5. Cunningham, 11.

6. Cunningham, 11.

7. Edain McCoy, as quoted on the website ReligiousTolerance.org, www.religioustolerance .org.

8. Kenneth Boa, "All About Eve: Feminism and the Meaning of Equality," www.bible.org.

9. Cunningham, 11.

10. Cunningham, 18-19.

11. Cunningham, 13.

12. Cunningham, 15.

13. Starhawk, "A Working Definition of Reclaiming," www.reclaiming.org/about/directions/definition.html.

Chapter 7—The Feminine Factor

1. Carol Christ, *Rebirth of the Goddess: Finding Meaning in Feminist Spirituality* (New York: Routledge, 1997), xiii.

2. Catherine Edwards Sanders, "Weak Church, Wiccan Charms," *Prism*, November/December 2005. See www.catherinesanders.com/writings.html.

3. Personal story shared on Facebook. Used with permission. Name has been changed.

4. The U.S. Army's *A Handbook for Chaplains*, 231-36.

5. Maplecrow, "A Pagan in the Workplace," The Witches' Voice (www.witchvox.com). Posted on December 16, 2007. Accessed on December 29, 2007. Used by permission.

6. Catherine Edwards Sanders, *Wicca's Charm* (Colorado Springs: Shaw Books, 2005), xi.

7. From a personal interview by Marla Alupoaicei. Used with permission.

8. Margot Adler, as quoted by Sanders in *Wicca's Charm*, 49.

9. Sanders, "Weak Church, Wiccan Charms."

10. Sanders, *Wicca's Charm*, 74-75.

Chapter 8—"I Was a Witch"

1. This article first appeared in *Today's Christian Woman*, September/October 2002, 38. Used with permission. To obtain an electronic copy, see www.christianitytoday.com/tcw/2002/sepoct/20.38.html?start=1.

Chapter 9—Compassion for Creation

1. Steven James, *Story: Recapture the Mystery* (Grand Rapids, MI: Revell, 2006), 19.

2. Raymond Buckland, *Teen Witch Datebook* (St. Paul, MN: Llewellyn Publications, 2002), 4.

3. The Wheel of the Year, from "The Witches of Oz" by Julia Phillips and Matthew Sandow, Sydney, New South Wales. See www.ladyoftheearth.com/wicca/wicca-19.txt.

4. Rudyard Kipling, *Kim*, chapter 6, as quoted in the Wiccan Book of Shadows. See http://ebooks.adelaide.edu.au/k/kipling/rudyard/kim/chapter6.html.

5. From a personal interview by Marla Alupoaicei. Used with permission.

6. The Wheel of the Year.

7. Reclaiming, www.reclaiming.org.

8. Reclaiming, "2008 WitchCamps," www.reclaiming.org. Also see www.witchcamp.org.

9. Starhawk, "A Working Definition of Reclaiming," www.reclaiming.org/about/directions/definition.html.

10. Patrick Meighan, "Spiral Scouts Based in Pagan Beliefs, Including Respect for Nature, People," *The Telegraph of Nashua*, 26 November 2002, www.nashuatelegraph.com. Also see www.religionnewsblog.com.

11. Meighan.

Chapter 10—"Mom, Today Someone Cast a Spell on Me!"

1. Alex Mar, quoted at www.teenwitch.com.

2. Katy Abel, "Wicca: Many Girls Find It Spellbinding," FamilyEducation.com. Accessed at http://life.familyeducation.com/occult/religion/36520.html.

3. Catherine Edwards Sanders, *Wicca's Charm* (Colorado Springs: Shaw Books, 2005), 97.

4. "Religious Clothing and Jewelry in School," ReligiousTolerance.org. Accessed at www.religious tolerance.org/sch_clot5.htm. See also www.religioustolerance.org/sch_clot2.htm.

5. Cited at www.religioustolerance.org/sch_clot.htm.

6. Abel.

7. Neela Banerjee, "Wiccans Keep the Faith with a Religion under Wraps," *New York Times*, 16 May 2007. Accessed at www.nytimes.com/2007/05/16/us/16wiccan.html?_r=2&oref =slogin&pagewanted=print.

8. Patti Wigington, "My Parents Don't Want Me to Be Wiccan—Can't I Just Lie?" About.com. Accessed at http://paganwiccan.about.com/od/faq/f/parents.htm.

9. "How Do I Tell My Parents?" Witchvox.com, May 5, 2001. Accessed at www.witchvox .com/va/dt_va.html?a=usor&c=teen&id=3420.

Chapter 11—"My Roommate Is a Witch...Really!"

1. Peter Wood, "Strange Gods: Neo-Paganism on Campus," *National Review*, 5 September 2001. Accessed at www.nationalreview.com/comment/comment-wood090501.shtml.

2. Online at www.apocalypse.org/pub/u/hilda/collpgn.html.

3. See www.pluralism.org.

4. See www.msupagans.com.

5. See www.circlesanctuary.org/studies/academicnetwork.htm.

6. See www.circlesanctuary.org/media/.

7. Alan Cooperman, "Fallen Soldier Gets a Bronze Star but No Pagan Star," *Washington Post*, 4 July 2006, A02.

8. Jami Shoemaker, as quoted by Catherine Edwards Sanders in *Wicca's Charm* (Colorado Springs: Shaw Books, 2005), 101.

9. http://lamar.colostate.edu/~csupsa/index.htm.

10. http://www.umaine.edu/paco/.

11. Kathleen Weresynski, "Wicca Casts Spell Over College Students," *Fox News*, 12 December 2002. Accessed at http://www.foxnews.com/story/0,2933,72791,00.html.

12. Weresynski.

Chapter 12—Emblems of Belief

1. Randy Meyers, "Military Casts Wicca in the Shadows," *Contra Costa Times*, 12 August 2004. See www.religionnewsblog.com.

2. Alan Cooperman, "The Army Chaplain Who Wanted to Switch to Wicca? Transfer Denied," *Washington Post*, 19 February 2007. See www.religionnewsblog.com.

3. Scott Bauer, "Wiccans Demand Acceptance," *USA Today*, 21 December 2006. See www
.usatoday.com.

4. Military Pagan Network, www.milpagan.org/advocacy/index.html.

5. Military Pagan Network, www.milpagan.org/resources/glossary.html.

6. Herne, www.wicca.com/celtic/wicca/military.htm.

7. "Wiccan Lawsuit's Goal: Acceptance," AP, via the *New York Times*, 21 December 2006.

8. Cooperman.

9. Meyers.

10. Meyers.

11. Katie McDaniel, as quoted by Jennifer H. Svan in "Military Pagans Struggle for Acceptance," *Stars and Stripes*, 12 June 2007. See www.military.com.

12. Lord Anord Iontach, "Pagans in Arms—Proper Actions for Military Pagans," posted 25 September 2005. See www.witchvox.com.

13. Steve Matrazzo, "Wicca Is Stepping Out of the Shadows," *Dundalk Eagle*, 26 July 2007. See www.religionnewsblog.com.

14. Frostig, "Military Pagans in Baghdad," posted 27 August 2006. See www.witchvox.com. Used with permission.

15. Frostig. Used with permission.

Chapter 13—Engaging the Seeker

1. Darrell Bock, from the "Jesus in Prime Time" conference, 2007. Bock is Professor of New Testament Studies, Dallas Theological Seminary.

2. Neela Banerjee, "Wiccans Keep the Faith With a Religion Under Wraps," *New York Times*, 16 May 2007. See www.nytimes.com/2007/05/16/us/16wiccan.html?_r=1&th&emc =th&oref=slogin.

3. Banerjee.

4. Banerjee.

5. Madeleine L'Engle, "Healed, Whole and Holy," from *Walking on Water: Reflections on Faith and Art* (Wheaton, IL: Harold Shaw Publishers, 1980). See http://greenbelt.com/news/ aslan/lengle.htm.

6. Steven James, *Story: Recapture the Mystery* (Grand Rapids, MI: Revell, 2006), 80-81.

7. Marla Alupoaicei, "Jesus as the Word," as quoted in the forthcoming book *Flow* (Ventura, CA: Regal Books, 2009).

8. From a survey of postmoderns by George Barna.

9. A few points on the attributes of postmoderns were adapted from Mary DeMuth's excellent book *Authentic Parenting in a Postmodern Culture* (Eugene, OR: Harvest House Publishers, 2007), 24-26.

10. Roger Dobson and Lauren Veevers, "Witchcraft Casts Spell on Young," *The Independent*, 20 May 2007.

11. Margot Adler, as quoted on the website ReligiousTolerance.org, www.religioustolerance .org/witchcra.htm.

Chapter 14—Knowing the Truth

1. Scott Cunningham, *The Truth About Witchcraft Today* (St. Paul, MN: Llewellyn Publications, 1999), 77.

2. Philip S. Johnson, "Wiccans and Christians: Some Mutual Challenges," Jesus.com.au. Accessed at www.jesus.com.au/html/page/false_witness.

3. Portions of this section have been adapted from John Ankerberg and Dillon Burroughs, *What's the Big Deal About Other Religions?* (Eugene, OR: Harvest House Publishers, 2008).

4. Johnson, "Wiccans and Christians: Some Mutual Challenges."

5. Additional verses include Exodus 22:18; Isaiah 8:19; 19:1-4; 44:24-25; and Hosea 4:12.

6. We realize that the events related in this passage have several interpretations. But the emphasis here remains focused on the fact that Saul was condemned for seeking counsel through a spirit guide and with the spirits of the dead.

7. Gwydion Oak, "How to Share the Gospel with Pagans," Witchvox.com, February 2, 1997. Accessed at www.witchvox.com/va/dt_va.html?a=usxx&c=words&id=1946.

8. Oak.

Chapter 15—How Investigating Wicca Strengthened Our Faith

1. Philip S. Johnson, "Wiccans and Christians: Some Mutual Challenges," Jesus.com.au. Accessed at www.jesus.com.au/html/page/preface.

2. Catherine Edwards Sanders, *Wicca's Charm* (Colorado Springs: Shaw Books, 2005), 128.

If you would like to read more about Wicca and about how to approach those who choose this path, check out the following books.

Abanes, Richard. *Harry Potter and the Bible: The Menace Behind the Magick.* Petoskey, MI: Horizon Books, 2001.

———. *Harry Potter, Narnia, and The Lord of the Rings: What You Need to Know About Fantasy Books and Movies.* Eugene, OR: Harvest House Publishers, 2005.

Adler, Margot. *Drawing Down the Moon: Witches, Druids, Goddess-Worshippers, and Other Pagans in America Today,* revised and expanded edition. New York: Penguin Books, 1997.

Ankerberg, John, and Dillon Burroughs. *What's the Big Deal About Other Religions?* Eugene, OR: Harvest House Publishers, 2008.

Baker, Tim. *Dewitched.* Nashville: Transit Books, Thomas Nelson, 2004.

Bridger, Frances. *A Charmed Life: The Spirituality of Potterworld.* New York: Doubleday, Image Books, 2002.

Brooks, Keith, Irvine Robertson, and Dillon Burroughs. *Comparing Christianity with the Cults.* Chicago: Moody Publishers, 2007.

Buckland, Raymond. *Buckland's Complete Book of Witchcraft,* second ed. St. Paul, MN: Llewellyn Publications, 2002.

———. *Wicca for One: The Path of Solitary Witchcraft.* New York: Citadel Press, 2004.

Cantrell, Gary. *Wiccan Beliefs and Practices.* St. Paul, MN: Llewellyn Publications, 2006.

Cunningham, Scott. *Earth Power: Techniques of Natural Magic.* St. Paul, MN: Llewellyn Publications, 2002.

———. *Living Wicca: A Further Guide for the Solitary Practitioner.* St. Paul, MN: Llewellyn Publications, 2002.

———. *Wicca: A Guide for the Solitary Practitioner.* St. Paul, MN: Llewellyn Publications, 1993.

DeMuth, Mary. *Authentic Parenting in a Postmodern Culture*. Eugene, OR: Harvest House Publishers, 2007.

Drew, A.J. *Wicca for Couples: Making Magick Together*. Franklin Lakes, NJ: The Career Press, 2002.

Dunwich, Gerina. *The Wicca Spellbook: A Witch's Collection of Wiccan Spells, Potions, and Recipes*, new ed. New York: Citadel Press, 2000.

Farrar, Janet, and Stewart Farrar. *A Witches' Bible: The Complete Witches' Handbook*, new ed. Blaine, WA: Phoenix Publishing, 1996.

———. *Eight Sabbats for Witches*, rev. ed. Blaine, WA: Phoenix Publishing, 1988.

———. *The Witches' Way*. Blaine, WA: Phoenix Publishing, 1984.

Gallagher, Ann-Marie. *The Wicca Bible*. New York: Sterling Publishing Co., Inc., 2005.

Grimassi, Raven. *The Wiccan Mysteries: Ancient Origins and Teachings*. St. Paul, MN: Llewellyn Publications, 2000.

Holland, Eileen. *The Wiccan Handbook*. Boston: Weiser Books, 2000.

James, Steven. *Story: Recapture the Mystery*. Grand Rapids, MI: Revell, 2006.

Kimball, Dan. *They Like Jesus, but Not the Church*. Grand Rapids, MI: Zondervan, 2006.

Kinnaman, David. *unChristian: What a New Generation Really Thinks about Christianity and Why It Matters*. Grand Rapids, MI: Baker Books, 2007.

Miller, Donald. *Blue Like Jazz*. Nashville: Thomas Nelson, 2003.

Murphy-Hiscock, Arin. *Solitary Wicca for Life: A Complete Guide to Mastering the Craft on Your Own*. Avon, MA: Adams Media Corporation, 2005.

Neal, Connie. *The Gospel According to Harry Potter*. Louisville, KY: Westminster John Knox Press, 2002.

O'Brien, Michael. *A Landscape with Dragons*. San Francisco: Ignatius Press, 1998.

RavenWolf, Silver. *Teen Witch: Wicca for a New Generation*. St. Paul, MN: Llewellyn Publications, 2004.

———. *Solitary Witch: The Ultimate Book of Shadows for the New Generation*. St. Paul, MN: Llewellyn Publications, 2003.

————. *To Ride a Silver Broomstick: New Generational Witchcraft*, new ed. St. Paul, MN: Llewellyn Publications, 2002.

Russo, Steve. *Protecting Your Teen from Today's Witchcraft: A Parent's Guide to Confronting Wicca and the Occult*. Grand Rapids, MI: Baker Books, 2005.

————. *What's the Deal with Wicca?* Minneapolis: Bethany House Publishers, 2005.

Sabin, Thea. *Wicca for Beginners: Fundamentals of Philosophy and Practice*. St. Paul, MN: Llewellyn Publications, 2006.

Sanders, Catherine Edwards. *Wicca's Charm*. Colorado Springs: Shaw Books, 2005.

Starhawk. *The Spiral Dance: A Rebirth of the Ancient Religion of the Goddess*, twentieth anniversary ed. New York: HarperOne, 1999.

Starkey, Marion L. *The Devil in Massachusetts: A Modern Enquiry into the Salem Witch Trials*. New York: Anchor Books, 1989.

Valiente, Doreen. *The Rebirth of Witchcraft*. Blaine, WA: Phoenix Publishing, 1989.

Wohlberg, Steve. *Hour of the Witch*. Shippensburg, PA: Destiny Image, 2005.

Zimmermann, Denise, and Katherine A. Gleason, rev. with Miria Liguana. *The Complete Idiot's Guide to Wicca and Witchcraft*, third ed. New York: Alpha Books, 2006.

About the Authors

Marla Alupoaicei is a full-time author, editor, and poet whose writing has been featured in a variety of magazines and literary journals, including *Kindred Spirit; Marriage Partnership; Illya's Honey; 3.1.6.: A Journal of Christian Thinking; Writer's Digest;* and *Oberon.* Marla and her husband founded Leap of Faith Ministries to provide inspirational articles, transformational truth, and life-changing resources for authors, intercultural couples, and Christian artists. Marla enjoys mentoring young writers as well as speaking, taking mission trips, ministering to intercultural couples, attending writers' conferences, and studying photography and music. Marla is a graduate of Dallas Theological Seminary. She, her husband, and their four cats reside in Texas. You may contact Marla as follows:

Marla's website: **Leap of Faith** at **www.marriageleap.com**
Marla's e-mail: **marla_alupoaicei@yahoo.com**

Dillon Burroughs is a staff writer for the award-winning television and radio program *The John Ankerberg Show,* which is broadcast into over 185 countries. He is the author or coauthor of 14 books, including the popular *What Can Be Found in LOST?;* the newest edition of the Facts On series (with John Ankerberg and John Weldon—over 2 million sold); and the Comparing Christianity series (over 1 million sold). Dillon is a graduate of Dallas Theological Seminary and lives with his wife and two children in Tennessee. You can find out more about him or contact him as follows:

Dillon's website: **www.readdB.com** or **www.myspace.com/readdB**
Dillon's e-mail: **dillon@dillonburroughs.org**

Harvest House Helps
You Engage the Culture

WHAT CAN BE FOUND IN *LOST*?
John Ankerberg and Dillon Burroughs

In one of the most popular TV series of all time, the characters struggle with issues of identity, conflict, relationships, and spirituality. The authors offer practical suggestions to make *Lost* a useful "point of reference" for talking effectively to others about spiritual themes such as the selfish bent of human nature and the darkness of evil; the hunger people have for acceptance and success; and the realization of our need for hope and for God.

WHAT'S THE BIG DEAL ABOUT OTHER RELIGIONS?
John Ankerberg and Dillon Burroughs

With so many different religions, how can anyone know what to believe? The search for answers begins by going back to the basics—how these religions began, what they teach, and evaluating the validity of their claims. That's the goal of authors John Ankerberg and Dillon Burroughs as they share the core essentials about Christianity, Islam, Mormonism, Wicca, New Age religions, atheism, and many others.

Current research, comparative charts, and thoughtful analysis all work together to make this a valuable resource for those who desire clarity in their quest for truth.

THE TRUTH ABOUT JESUS AND THE "LOST GOSPELS"
A Reasoned Look at Thomas, Judas, and the Gnostic Gospels
David Marshall

Do the "Lost Gospels" unveil a side of Jesus we never knew? Recent headlines, bestselling books, and even a blockbuster movie have called a lot of attention to ancient documents that portray a Jesus far different from the one found in the Bible.

- What are the "Lost Gospels," and where did they come from?
- Are these writings trustworthy? Are they on par with the Bible?
- Have we had wrong perceptions about Jesus all along?

A careful comparison of the "Lost Gospels" to the Bible itself reveals discrepancies that are cause for concern. This eye-opening resource will enable you to take a well-informed and well-reasoned stand on an ongoing and crucial controversy.

HARVEST HOUSE PUBLISHERS

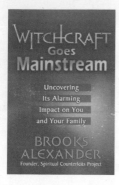

WITCHCRAFT GOES MAINSTREAM
Brooks Alexander

The Halloween witch is dead. The old crone on a broomstick is gone. In her place is a young, hip, sexually magnetic woman who worships a goddess and practices socially acceptable magic.

As witchcraft goes mainstream, this new image, or some other aspect of the rapidly growing pagan religious movement, shapes the identity of more and more of your co-workers and neighbors...perhaps even your friends and family members. What do you do or say when you or your children meet someone like this?

Brooks Alexander, founder of the Spiritual Counterfeits Project, pointedly answers the tough questions:

- What do modern witches believe? Are they really following ancient pagan traditions or worshipping the devil?

- What's the real history behind Wicca and neopaganism? How is today's witchcraft related to the past?

- How might these spiritual beliefs transform our culture in the future?

- What does the widespread acceptance of witchcraft mean for you right now?

- How can you respond to protect your loved ones and reach out with the love of Jesus?

Weighing our ever-changing spiritual surroundings within a biblical framework, Witchcraft Goes Mainstream will help you chart a course for yourself and your family and see the light of God more clearly in a darkening culture.

To read a sample chapter from this
or another Harvest House book, go to
www.harvesthousepublishers.com.